Praise for *Happiness Is an Inside Job*

"Sylvia Boorstein is an excellent teacher of Buddhist practice because she teaches from her own experiences of her own practice. Let us allow the teaching to water the seeds of compassion and wisdom in us so that our joy and happiness could grow every day. The book in your hand is highly enjoyable."

—THICH NHAT HANH, author of *Living Buddha, Living Christ*

"A small, polished gem of a book."

—*Publishers Weekly* (starred review)

"This refreshing book offers an honest, down-to-earth presentation of how mindfulness meditation actually works. With a nonsectarian approach animated by personal stories, *Happiness Is an Inside Job* will be of value to anyone who seeks to live in this world with greater self-awareness, sensitivity, and kindness."

—STEPHEN BATCHELOR, author of *Buddhism Without Beliefs*

"With wonderful stories from her own life and with memorable phrases to keep in mind through difficult times, Sylvia Boorstein demonstrates that all of us have the ability to become aware of our thought patterns, habits, and tendencies without being held hostage by them. This is a truly delightful book filled with simple wisdom for the journey."

—SARAH SUSANKA, author of *The Not So Big Life*

Also by Sylvia Boorstein

PAY ATTENTION, FOR GOODNESS' SAKE:
Practicing the Perfections of the Heart—
The Buddhist Path of Kindness

IT'S EASIER THAN YOU THINK:
The Buddhist Way to Happiness

DON'T JUST DO SOMETHING, SIT THERE:
A Mindfulness Retreat

THAT'S FUNNY, YOU DON'T LOOK BUDDHIST:
On Being a Faithful Jew and a Passionate Buddhist

Happiness

Is an Inside Job

Happiness

Is an Inside Job

PRACTICING FOR A JOYFUL LIFE

Sylvia Boorstein, Ph.D.

Ballantine Books   New York

2008 Ballantine Books Trade Paperback Edition

Copyright © 2007 by Sylvia Boorstein, Ph.D.

Published in the United States by Ballantine Books, an imprint of The Random House
Publishing Group, a division of Random House, Inc., New York.

BALLANTINE and colophon are registered trademarks of Random House, Inc.

Originally published in hardcover in the United States by Ballantine Books,
an imprint of The Random House Publishing Group,
a division of Random House, Inc., in 2007.

Library of Congress Cataloging-in-Publication Data
Boorstein, Sylvia.
Happiness is an inside job : practicing for a joyful life / Sylvia Boorstein.
p. cm.
Includes bibliographical references.
ISBN 978-0-345-48132-0 (trade pbk.)
1. Religious life—Buddhism.   2. Happiness—Religious aspects—Buddhism.
I. Title.
BQ5395.B66 2008
294.3'444—dc22   2007028325

Printed in the United States of America

www.ballantinebooks.com

2 4 6 8 9 7 5 3 1

Book design by Carol Malcolm Russo

IN MEMORY OF
MARTHA LOUISE LEY,
A VERY GOOD FRIEND TO MANY PEOPLE

Contents

Happiness

Is an Inside Job

INTRODUCTION

The Best Way to Live

I was sitting at my computer writing when my friend Martha called to say that her brother Jack's illness had just taken a turn for the much worse. I felt sad, mostly for Martha, whom I knew well, but also for her brother, a man I'd met, a person whose family I knew. I said what I hoped were consoling words. As soon as our conversation ended, I went back to writing, eager to resume because I'd had what I'd thought was a good idea just as the phone had rung. Then I realized I'd forgotten the point I was about to make, and I heard myself think, "So inconvenient of Jack to get worse just today." I felt my heart wince at the thought. Then I stopped.

I turned off the computer. I lit a candle. I sat in my rocking chair and looked out the window. I thought about Jack and his children and grandchildren. I thought about Martha, in her sixties, who often described herself as "Jack's baby sister," and about Martha's mother, almost ninety, facing the loss of her son. Pretty soon I found myself thinking about other people I knew who were suffering. I thought good wishes for them, individually for as long as I could keep up, and then collectively when I realized my list was enormous. I said the prayer phrases that are part of ritual *metta* (loving-kindness) practice, which end with "May all beings, everywhere, be happy and peaceful, and come to the end of suffering."

I felt better. I looked at the few late summer flowers still blooming on my deck outside my window. I thought about how fragile all life is and how quickly it passes. I was glad to be alive. I thought about my family—all, on that day, well—and felt fortunate. I thought about my friends who were well and prayed that they would thrive. I wished everyone I could think of well. At some point, I had the thought, "Go back and finish the writing," but no impulse arose in me to move. I felt peaceful, and very happy.

I love it that what my heart wants most to do is to console or appreciate or encourage. It feels better in relationship. I imagine it ever on the lookout for an object—a frightened friend, my own chagrined self, the world around me—that it can connect with. And I love it that it reminds me—tells me, "Turn off the computer. Light a candle. Pay attention"—even when, perhaps especially when, I seem not to be listening. I feel delighted to have been born into what the Buddha called "this realm of ten thousand joys and ten thousand woes" with mind and heart primed to respond, out of wisdom, and out of natural benevolence, with kindness. I thought, "This is the best way to live." I also thought about how easily my mind forgets what it knows, how easily it falls into confusion and out of caring connection. So I decided to write this book—not about avoiding confusion, because we can't—but about becoming unconfused and restoring connection because it really is the best way to live.

Restoring the Mind to Kindness

I wish it were true that regular meditation and prayer guaranteed equanimity, but it's not that way for me. I began to practice mindfulness in 1977, and I meditate and pray and study and teach, and I still get angry or worried or impatient or frightened. The difficulties—great and small—of my regular life present ongoing challenges to peace of mind. I feel annoyed when my personal plans don't work out, and I often feel chagrined and dismayed when I see that my personal plans are taking up so much space in my mind when the world is in such terrible trouble. I'm also continually surprised to find how the pains of my past—shame, sadness, guilt, losses, fears of even long, long ago—remain easily activated sensitivities that upset my heart all over again through memory. A grandchild, coughing the benign cough of a child turning over in bed in the next room, frightens me out of a sleep because the sound matches the sound of my mother coughing the cough of congestive heart failure in a bedroom down the hall from me sixty years ago, and I wake up sad.

I've gotten over being surprised that my internal life isn't more smooth and peaceful than it is. I think I imagined, when I began meditating, that I'd become much more tranquil than I am. In the years since I've begun teaching Buddhist Concentration and Mindfulness meditations, I've often had students ask me how it feels to be peaceful all the time. I am eager to tell them that although I think I am wiser about the decisions that I make, and generally kinder, I am not peaceful all the time. By temperament, I am somewhat dramatic, and personality doesn't change. I remain a passionate person. What happens in my family and what happens in the world are both important to me. I can't imagine not being cheered by good news or saddened by bad news. I wouldn't want it otherwise. I feel alive when I know that I care, that things matter. Although it is true that feeling cheered and saddened need not *necessarily* upset the mind's balance, for me—perhaps because I startle easily—they often do.

Still, I consider my meditation practice a success because of one crucial and definite change in me in the thirty years since I began. I now trust that even when what is happening to me is difficult and my response to it is painful, I will not suffer if I can keep my mind clear enough to keep my heart engaged. I know that my suffering begins whenever my mind, for whatever reason—the enormity or the suddenness of the challenge, its own exhausted state—becomes confused. In its confusion, it seems to forget everything it ever knew. It tells itself stories, alternatively angry ("This isn't fair!") or pitiful ("Poor me!") or frightening ("I can't *stand* it if things aren't different!"). No inner voice of wisdom ("This *is* what is happening, it's part of the whole spectrum of painful things that happen to human beings, and you *can* manage") can make itself heard to soothe the distress. I continue to suffer, stumbling around in stories of discontent, until I catch myself, and stop, and allow myself to know, and deeply feel, that I am frightened or confused or disappointed or angry or tired or ashamed or sad—that

"I'm in pain!" Then my own good heart, out of compassion, takes care of me. It all happens when I am able to say to myself (I honestly do use these very words), "Sweetheart, you are in pain. Relax. Take a breath. Let's pay attention to what is happening. Then we'll figure out what to do."

In those rescue phrases, there are three instructions.

The first is "Relax." This is a startling instruction— "Relax? Are you kidding? I'm upset!"—to give to a mind held captive by confusing and dismaying stories. It's the startle, though, that matters. It interrupts the stories. It isn't the instruction for *how* to calm down, but it is the reminder that calming down is possible. It inspires the next instruction, which is "Breathe."

We are always breathing, of course, but this instruction means, "Pay *attention* to your breath. Put all of your awareness into this next breath, the next few breaths." Attending particularly to the breath accomplishes two things. First of all, because the breath becomes shallow and the body becomes tense when the mind is disturbed, lengthening the breath calms the body. Second, and more important, it causes the mind, for the space of time it's attending to breath, noticing it in descriptive terms, to drop the story line of discontent. We can multitask, but we can't advance two story lines at the same time. The narrative accompaniment to attentive breathing, "I'm breathing in a long breath" or "I am breathing in a shallow breath" or "I am breathing in a whatever kind of breath," is a straightforward description of a current reality, and its neutrality calms the mind. It replaces the alarming, non-neutral "Woe is me" narrative of the mind in contention with experience. Concentrating the attention on one neutral focus, such as the breath, calms the mind and begins to clear it of confusing energies. Even a small moment of clarity reminds the mind it could possibly choose a helpful response. That awareness provides hope and courage. (Saying "Take a breath" is a generic shortcut. Any neutral focus would work. A substitute for breath, a blessing phrase repeated aloud or spoken silently, also calms the mind, and since I use them a lot, they will be part of this book.) Calming the mind prepares it for the last instruction, "Pay attention to what's happening."

Pay attention, in other words, to the presence of distress and, if it is obvious, to what prompted it. "I am mad because he said . . ." Or "I am terribly ashamed because I just remembered . . ." Or "I am overwhelmed by the pain of the world. . . ." Or "My best friend just met the love of his life, and I am jealous. . . ." Or "My best friend is dying, and I'm afraid I won't have heart enough to support her." The most important instruction, always, is "Pay attention to the feeling of distress." Sometimes the proximal cause is obvious, sometimes not. It doesn't matter. Pain is pain. Knowing the story of the distress is helpful for choosing a response, but my first response—in addition to the recognition of the pain—is to not be mad at it, or at myself for falling into it. That's why it's important that I say, "Sweetheart." (You might use another word, if that one doesn't work for you, as long as it means that you aren't mad at yourself for whatever difficult feeling is present.) "Sweetheart" reminds me that it isn't my fault that my mind is embittered, that something has upset it, that I'm in pain. Even if I see that the source of my suffering is my own mind's refusing to accommodate to its challenge, I can still feel compassionate about that. No one purposely suffers. If I could peacefully accommodate, I would. This is a book about restoring the mind to its natural wisdom and kindness, to its capacity for caring connection, whenever confusion overwhelms it into suffering.

The Heart of Buddhist Teachings:
Wise Effort, Wise Mindfulness, Wise Concentration

We'll start, as the Buddha did in his declaration of what is fundamentally true about life, with the premise that challenges in life are inevitable and that suffering, the mind in contentious mode with its experience, is the instinctive response of the untrained mind. These premises are the first two of the famous Four Noble Truths regarded as the summation of the Buddha's teaching. The third truth is the definite promise that a peaceful mind, one not in contention with anything, is a possibility for human beings. This doesn't mean a mind that likes everything or condones everything or even is indifferent to everything. It means a mind that has come to understand that contention produces (indeed, *is*) suffering. It means a mind able, through clarity, to choose a wise response. The fourth truth is the Buddha's training program for developing that kind of mind. The training program has eight parts (hence, the Eightfold Path), all of which are designed to cultivate equanimity, the balance in the mind that sustains both natural wisdom and the natural inclination to love.

My dedication to meditation practice is inspired by the promise that this kind of equanimity is possible. I want to live my life wisely, not in contention with anything, able to love. This sounds quite ordinary to me as I write it, but I think it's the fundamental goal of spiritual practice. Or of life, really. I want to feel safe and peaceful, and I also want to be interested in and passionately engaged with the world.

Here is a classic Buddhist image that I bring to mind— quite often, actually—to remind me of what is possible. It's the scene of the Buddha sitting under the bodhi tree on the night of his enlightenment, absolutely resolute, determined to free his mind from all confusion. I see him as he is described in the texts, in classic cross-legged pose, one palm resting upward in his lap, the fingers of his other hand touching the earth in front of him. According to legend, Mara, the personification of evil, arrives at that very moment to thwart his plan. Accompanying Mara are all the forces that confuse the mind. The Buddha, recognizing the temptations that are about to assail him, is said to have proclaimed, "I see your armies, Mara, and I am not afraid!" (I love the phrase "I am not afraid!" Maybe it's the best phrase we can say, other than "I have everything I need." Maybe they are the same.)

Visualize, if you can, the rest of the scene as legends describe it: The forces of Mara unleash spears and arrows in the direction of the Buddha and assail him with frightening images. He sits poised, equanimous. The spears and arrows turn into flowers as they encounter the field of benevolence that surrounds the Buddha, and they fall on the ground around him. Mara then creates a display of erotic temptations. Their allure is diffused by the radiant ease surrounding the Buddha. The vanquished Mara disappears. By the first light of morning, the Buddha proclaims his full understanding.

In this legend, the Buddha gains access to wisdom because he is peaceful. He abides, alert, and insight arises. Equanimity is portrayed as a prerequisite for liberation. For me, the image of the Buddha maintaining his equanimity in the face of challenge is itself a metaphor for liberation. I think that the Buddha's wisdom, already complete in its understanding that struggle is suffering, is what allows him to choose peace. I think that his deep understanding of karma, his certainty that things come to pass when the necessary and sufficient conditions have been met, enables him to remain tranquil as events unfold. I think of the protective field that surrounds him—in the story, transforming potentially afflictive blows into flowers—as being his unshakable benevolence, the external reflection of his equanimity.

If I were to write a one-sentence caption for the image of the Buddha vanquishing Mara, it would be: Steadfast benevolence, sustained by the wisdom that anything other than benevolence is painful, protects the mind from all afflictions.

I am inspired by the fact that the Buddha was a human being. That makes it possible for me to imagine that I could also cultivate wisdom and benevolence. I know that legends say that the Buddha had many, many previous lifetimes of preparation for his moment under the bodhi tree. I feel reassured by that, not daunted. I make the analogy that I must also be bringing the accumulated wisdom of my past experiences to each new situation. We all do. And I am inspired by knowing that the Buddha is said to have placed his hand on the ground as Mara appeared, in a gesture that signified, "I have a right to be here." I believe that we also have the right—the "right" of human beings with elaborate minds— to recognize challenge, to choose to override the instinctive impulses of flight or fight, to act in ways that keep the peace inside us and create peace around us. I know it is a skill that needs to be learned, and not a simple one, but the fact that it's a possibility supports the courage I bring to my practice.

I've chosen the three meditative steps, the "mind-training steps," of the Eightfold Path—Wise Effort, Wise Mindfulness, and Wise Concentration—as the focus of this book. In traditional texts, the list of the path steps begins with Wise Action, Wise Speech, and Wise Livelihood, morality trainings that present our relationships with others as a means of cultivating wisdom. The list ends with Wise Understanding and Wise Aspiration, often called wisdom trainings, which I experience as the cultivation of the faith that peace is possible and the determination to achieve it. Wise Effort, Wise Mindfulness, and Wise Concentration are the middle three steps of the Eightfold Path, and I've come to think of them as, figurative and literally, the heart of the path. All of the path parts depend on one another, and they all support the development of equanimity and the sustaining of wisdom, but I've made the choice to emphasize the meditative steps for two reasons.

The first reason is philosophical. I am committed to the idea that equanimity in the mind is the foundation of wisdom and that wisdom sustains the mind's capacity to respond with benevolence. Effort, concentration, and mindfulness are the internal ways in which the mind restores itself from being out of balance and lost in confusion to a condition of ease, clarity, and wisdom. No external action needs to happen. No recourse to wisdom—which isn't present when the mind is confused—needs to be available. The return to wisdom is an inside job.

The second reason is practical and personal. My experience, over time, is that my meditation practice has changed my mind. Although I remain familiar to my friends and my style of being is much the same as ever, the habits of my mind, the thoughts and feelings that my mind generates that only I know about, are different. I worry less. I am more tolerant, less judgmental, both of myself and of other people. Most important, I am more able to recognize when my mind has gotten itself into trouble and increasingly eager to mobilize the energy to rescue it. Concentration and mindfulness, as remedies to confusion, are either self-activating or, in more difficult times, at least reasonably easily available remedies to confusion. I still get upset, and sometimes confused, but I get over it sooner.

Wise Effort, the moment-to-moment discrimination practice meant to direct the attention in its choice of focus, seems to me the pivotal practice of all three meditative path steps. I think of it as the unsung, or undersung, hero of the whole of the Eightfold Path. It's the impulse to reroute the mind as it is falling (or if it has already fallen) into confusion. It's what initiates the awareness "You are in pain, sweetheart. Do something about it. Concentrate. Get a grip. Figure out what is happening. Choose a helpful response. This is not the direction in which you want to continue!" Without this "wake-up call," nothing would happen.

Although I'll talk about them separately, the truth is that Wise Effort and Mindfulness and Concentration aren't really three separate things. They are integral to one another. For the purposes of this book, I'll sometimes tell stories emphasizing one or another of them to make a point. For example, in order to show how concentration works to settle the mind, to ground it in some composure so that the work of mindfulness—understanding what is happening—can proceed, I'll give examples that highlight particular qualities of concentration. I'm aware as I do that, that the motivation to concentrate needs to be preceded by some wise effort, an attempt to replace a confused, uncomfortable mind state with one that is clearer. Also, that the moment of wise effort needs to be preceded by at least enough mindfulness to initiate the effort. Perhaps the formula is: a little mindfulness allows for the awareness of discomfort, which leads to intention to end discomfort, which leads to effort, which inspires concentration, which creates some composure, which allows for more mindfulness, which brings more clarity along with less discomfort, all of which lead to even more effort, more concentration, more mindfulness, more contentment, on and on, without beginning and without end in response to the regularly occurring challenges of life. It's not a mistake that contentment doesn't get established once and for all. Life is an ongoing series of changing circumstances to which human beings are continually called upon to respond. What the Buddha taught is that we could respond happily.

It feels important to me to say this up front and talk about all three mind-training practices as a trio that functions together, even if I tell stories that seem to present them individually and teach practices that purport to cultivate them as separate capacities. They are, in fact, three aspects of the process that reestablishes equanimity in the mind so that wisdom (uncommonly good sense) is restored and goodwill (the emotional counterpart of wisdom as well as the natural inclination of most human beings) can flourish.

Also, even as I present practices that are cultivated through meditation, I'll emphasize, as I always do when I teach, that effort, mindfulness, and concentration are every-day, whole-life, all-the-time practices. Often, someone will ask, when I say that, "Surely you don't go around all day monitoring your breathing or reciting blessings? How could you work? How could you have a life?"

I respond by saying that practicing one hundred percent of the time does not require any time. I do not spend my life noticing my breath or reciting blessings. I simply try to stay unconfused, and when I am confused, I try to do something about it. And I know whether or not I am confused most readily by noticing—being mindful of—my capacity for feeling caring concern. It is certainly true for me, and I think for most of us, that when I feel myself in caring connection—encouraging, consoling, or appreciating—I feel the twin pleasures of clarity and goodness. It doesn't matter if the connection I feel is to myself or a person I know or people I don't know or even the whole world. The lively impulse of caring is what counts.

So here is the ongoing question that is my gauge for measuring my level of confusion. "In this moment, am I able to care?" Not "Am I pleased?" There are all sorts of things I don't like. And in response to what I find unpleasant, I often feel dismayed or impatient or annoyed or disappointed or grieved. What I try to do is keep my mind from fighting with my experience, confusing and isolating itself in self-centered despair. The contentious mind is, by definition, confused. It hasn't remembered that struggle creates suffering and graceful response creates clarity. I am trying to stay unconfused and connected to my own kindness. Whenever I do, I relax, see what my options are, and choose the best of them. I won't always be pleased, but I'll be happy.

EQUANIMITY, WISDOM, AND KINDNESS

No One to Blame:
How Equanimity Inspires Wisdom

It's always good to start with a story.

I was wending my way slowly, along with hundreds of people, back and forth through the cordoned-off lanes of an airport security line, when I became aware of the conversation of the two people right behind me:

"It's your fault!"

"What do you mean, 'It's your fault'? It's *your* fault!"

"That's what I mean. It's your fault we're late."

"No, it's not. Prove it to me that it's my fault."

"I don't have to prove anything to you. It just is."

I glanced behind me, as if looking beyond them, and saw

that they were young, casually dressed, and apparently (was it tennis rackets, golf gear?) were going on holiday together.

The Ping-Pong recriminations continued. "Your fault." "No, yours."

I had a momentary impulse to turn around and say, "Listen to me! It does not matter one bit whose fault it is. Either you'll be in time for your flight or you won't. And if you miss this flight, there will be others. What's more, you don't know that this flight is the best one to be on. Perhaps this one will have engine trouble and the next one will arrive safely. Relax! You are ruining the beginning of your holiday with a useless skirmish."

Of course, I didn't say anything. I think I could have gotten away with it if I had done it sweetly enough, but I imagined them telling someone later, "You won't believe what this wacky little old woman in the airport . . ." Anyway, eavesdropping and intruding are both impolite, even if unintended and well meaning.

I took off my jacket and shoes and pushed them through the X-ray machine along with my carry-on bag with my computer out for inspection. Retrieving my possessions on the other side, balancing on one foot and then the other to hurriedly put on my shoes, I noticed the couple just in front of me, also just emerged through the sensor gate, taking a moment to kiss each other, give each other a hug. I was amused by the thought that they were congratulating each other for having made it through the security hurdle unscathed. It was the briefest of exchanges of affection, but it was there. Right in the middle of getting re-dressed. Then I thought, "I should call the attention of the arguing folks behind me to the kissing folks in front of me. 'Look,' I could tell them, 'here is another possibility. In fact, there are only two possibilities in any moment. You can kiss or you can fight. Kissing is better.' "

Of course, I said nothing and went on to my flight. I also knew then, as I know now as I write, that in situations where I feel stressed, I might behave like the couple behind me. Not even "long ago, when I wasn't wise," but right now, when I presumably understand that struggling with anything to make it be other than what it is creates suffering. If my mind becomes confused, broadsided by a challenge that upsets it, even a "minor" one such as "I'll miss my plane," I forget, at least for a while, what I know.

Becoming wise means, for me, forgetting less often— and remembering sooner when I've forgotten—the three things that are fundamentally true. The Buddha called these the Three Characteristics of Experience.

Everything is always changing.

There is a cause-and-effect lawfulness that governs all unfolding experience.

What I do matters, but I am not in charge. Suffering results from struggling with what is beyond my control.

The line from the *Dhammapada,* a compilation of sayings attributed to the Buddha, that sums this up for me, that seems the one-sentence best expression of wisdom, is: "Anyone who understands impermanence, ceases to be contentious."

Does that make sense to you on as many levels as it does to me? I understand it, primarily, as meaning "I have only a certain span of life allotted to me, so I don't want to waste a single moment of it fighting." Other times, if I catch myself on the brink of contention, the instruction reminds me, "Whatever is happening will change, and what I add to this situation is part of the change. Agonizing makes it worse." And sometimes, if I remember that whatever is happening will cause results that I really cannot anticipate (although I often do and worry needlessly), I say to myself, "I have no idea whether this changed circumstance, which I resent, is actually a good or a bad thing in the long run. I can wait to see."

Many people have told me, when I've asked for examples of wise people in their lives, "My granddad [or grandmother or elderly neighbor of my childhood or eighth-grade math teacher] always said, 'You do the best you can, and then you live with what happens. What else can you do?' "

I think in these descriptions of wisdom, the important word is *always*. Those wise people *always* said . . . They did not forget. I forget. I know—I think we all do from innumerable events in our experience—that the moment in which the mind acknowledges "This isn't what I wanted, but it's what I got" is the point at which suffering disappears. Sadness might remain present, but the mind, having given up the fight for another reality, is free to console, free to support the mind's acceptance of the situation, free to allow space for new possibilities to come into view.

My own experience is that I keep learning this lesson, over and over again. My wisdom is definitely not unshakable. Here is an example, from all too recent an experience. I became distracted, and . . . Well, here is the story, which speaks for itself.

I went to the antique store in the town in France where I live part of each year to protest the unexpected 400-euro charge that had arrived along with the mattress and innerspring for the bed I'd bought there. I had telephoned in advance. Madame Blaise, the *antiquaire,* had explained that, unfortunately, the unique size of beds made in the 1840s, especially the rounded corners, had required that a special-order mattress and springs be constructed. I was going in person to continue the discussion, but I was unhappy about going. I am, by nature, conflict-avoidant. I was urged on and accompanied by my husband, Seymour, who was angry and who does not speak French. I was caught between trying to please him and trying not to displease Madame Blaise.

"Remind her," he said, "that she told us what the price of the mattress would be, that it was included with the bed, and that we already paid for it. If there is anything extra, she should pay. She is the expert. It is her responsibility."

"Madame is an eighty-five-year-old small-town *antiquaire*," I countered. "She is not Macy's. You can't undo these things."

"It's not fair, though," he continued. "You should insist that she make amends. If you won't do it, I will. I'll pantomime how unhappy I am. Even if she won't give us any money back, she could at least offer us something like those bedside tables you were looking at when we bought the bed."

I spoke to Madame Blaise in my most elegant and polite French, explaining our shock, our dismay, and our distress about having trusted her judgment and now needing to pay the mattress company 400 euros. I looked pointedly at some of the furniture around us and suggested that she might consider making us a gift of bedside tables as a form of reparation. I ended by saying that we had enjoyed our previous meetings with her and were sad that we were now left with bad feelings, *mauvaises émotions*.

"Oh, madame," she responded, suddenly looking genuinely concerned and leaning toward me as if to reach out and comfort me. "*Mauvaises émotions* are very bad for you. You should put them down. Forget about it. It's in the past. These things happen. Really, *vraiment, mauvaises émotions* are very bad for you."

I wasn't surprised. Even if I was a bit chagrined about having fussed at all, and disappointed about not getting a consolation gift, I was tickled by how correct Madame Blaise was in her advice to me. Bad feelings *aren't* good for you. The Buddha taught, twenty-five hundred years ago, that anger is "a toxin in the veins." Modern mainstream magazines are saying the same thing. I see, when I am in France, that the word *stress* has made it into the language and the advice in health-related articles is "Ne stressez pas!"

Madame Blaise's instructions for what my unhappy-looking husband and I might do to get over our upset were exactly right. I felt myself relax, even as she lectured us. Think about what she said.

"You should put them [these *mauvaises émotions*] down." Of course we should have put them down. Being mad was uncomfortable for both of us. The thing is, when the mind feels wounded, it goes over the script incessantly, trying to validate the anger: "I said . . ." "She said . . ." "She promised . . ." "It's not fair . . ." Struggling with what we cannot change, the Buddha taught, creates suffering. And a friend of mine says that the words *It's not fair* have caused more trouble than any other words throughout history.

My sense of my mind when it gets stuck in a groove of resentment is that it's attempting to write a different end on the story, or else rehearse the error it made that caused the resentment to happen so that it wouldn't do it again. Both those goals, if you consider them, are futile. Things are what they are. Ruminating won't change them. Nor will it provide an insurance policy for avoiding pain in the future. In fact, it perpetuates it. Replaying upsetting experiences keeps the mind inflamed. Soothing the mind by giving the argument a rest is a better idea. That fits with the suggestion that I "forget about it," or at least "try to forget about it." The Buddha's advice, in verse 4 of the *Dhammapada,* is "Abandon such thoughts [resentment over having been abused, mistreated] and live in love."

On that day in France, caught in a confusion of thoughts that included "Why did I buy that stupid bed that has cost so much and made this trouble?" I continued the drama of protest until Madame Blaise reminded me, firmly, of what I had forgotten. Her final parry, "These things happen," was the best. *Everything* happens. Some things desirable, some not. You do the best with what you have. The irony of the moment was not lost on me. I thought, "I am supposed to know this."

When we left the store, after Madame Blaise and I had exchanged cordial wishes, Seymour said, "What did she say?"

I replied, "What she said, more or less, was 'That's life.' Let's go to the lamp store and look at end tables."

We Understand *and* We Feel: Warm Wisdom

I want to go back to the assertion I made earlier that "wisdom sustains the mind's capacity to respond with benevolence." I think it works in two ways. First of all, wisdom supports the mind in accepting that things are the way they are as a result of everything else in the world being the way it ever was and now is—this is the truth of interdependence, remember?—so that nothing, in *this* moment, can be otherwise. Knowing, positively, that the struggle to create a different current reality is to no avail helps keep the attention present even when experience is painful. And second, the same wisdom that keeps the attention alert and present in painful circumstances includes the awareness—because it is our *own* experience at that moment—that human beings *feel* about things, that we lament or yearn or grieve *even* when we understand that things can't be different. Life is a "no way out" situation. Moving through it means accommodating, often surrendering, and—somehow or other—managing how we feel.

Here's a classic Buddhist story: A distraught mother, carrying her son who has died, pleads with the Buddha to use his magical powers to restore her child to life. The Buddha assures the woman that he will revive the boy if she can provide a mustard seed from a home in which no one has ever died. When the mother returns from her fruitless search—death is ubiquitous, it visits every home—her frenzy has been replaced by wise surrender, and she becomes a devotee and student of the Buddha.

I am always touched by this story and its message of the calming potential of wisdom, but I often wish there had been one more detail, just one more sentence at the end of it. I invite you to think of what sentence, if any, you might add, and I'll also tell you—as a clue to what my sentence is—about my recent visit to a local retirement home, because both stories share a common theme.

A woman named Tova, a congregant at the synagogue I belong to and a resident of a local retirement home, had invited me to speak at the weekly meeting of the Library Club. We were arranging the chairs in a circle so we could begin when one of the dozen or so people in the group noticed a man standing in the doorway.

"Come on in," she said. "We're just getting ready to start."

"A woman down the hall," he said, pointing behind him, "just had a heart attack."

"Just come in," someone else urged. "You can't do anything about that."

"They've called the paramedics," the man added.

"That's good, then," another person said. "They'll know what to do. Come in."

I could see, through the glass double-door entrance to the library, people with serious faces and determined strides going in and out of a room down the hall. I'd realized, as I'd walked down that hall to the library, that the rooms on either side had hospital beds in them and windows as part of their walls so that the nursing staff could easily monitor the people in the beds. This was clearly the hospital wing of the retirement center, the facility for residents who became too sick to live on their own. The people with me in the library were the "independent-livers," people still able to maintain themselves in their own apartments in the large, surrounding, parklike development. I wondered what it would feel like to think, "I am in line for these very same rooms." The thought unnerved me.

The librarian began to introduce me. She specifically mentioned how much the group was looking forward to learning what the Buddha taught. As she spoke, I noticed three paramedics rolling a gurney past the door of the library.

"See?" the man who had been in the doorway, now seated in the group, pointed everyone's attention down the hall. "Paramedics."

"Happens every day," a woman said. "You get used to it."

"Do you?" I asked. "I'd really like to talk about that. The Buddha taught about the possibility of living peacefully, even happily, in full recognition that life is full of disappointments and losses and even big losses like death. What's it like," I asked, "to live in a place where the paramedics come every day?"

"It's fine," one of the few men in the room said in a tone that seemed to me to be an attempt to put a definitive end to this conversation. "Listen to me. There are nearly two hundred people living here. Old people die all the time. 'Carpe diem,' I say."

"Anyway," another woman added, "they usually don't put the siren on, so I don't know every time they come."

"The reason they don't put the siren on," someone else said, "is because most of the time, the person is already dead."

I could see, by glancing sideward through the glass doors, that there was still a lot of activity going on in the hall. It was hard not to look.

"How did you first get interested in Buddhism?" the librarian asked, hoping, I think, to get me back "on topic." I actually thought I *was* on topic. It was Siddhartha Gautama's realization of the inevitability of old age, sickness, and death, his understanding of the pain of all loss, that inspired him to leave his wife and child and life of comfort in search of a way to counter that pain. His declaration of the possibility of attaining a peaceful mind—a mind grounded in wisdom that recognizes challenge without creating suffering; indeed, a mind that attenuates suffering by responding with compassion—earned him the title of Buddha, the Enlightened One.

I was about to answer the "How did I get interested" question when the paramedics rolled the gurney back past the library in the direction of the front door. No one was on the gurney. I assumed the woman had died. I thought, "Maybe I should mention this. We could sit quietly for a while, offer prayers for the person who died, think about the people who will feel her loss." I hesitated. I was a visitor. I didn't know the local custom.

"Is Buddhism a religion or a philosophy?" someone asked. The question broke the spell of my musing.

"It is both," I said. I talked about the Buddha and about mindfulness. I gave some instructions for meditation and suggested that we all close our eyes and notice the experience of the breath coming in and out of our bodies. I explained how focusing on a simple repetitive event calms the mind.

We sat quietly. I tried to pay attention to my breath. Very soon the musing started again.

"Is this callous, or is this wise," I wondered, "this carrying on as if everything were normal? Someone just died down the hall. Is everyone here in denial? Or is it only I, startled by the immediacy of the death, who wants to stop and talk about it? Is the apparent ease of these people who see the paramedics so often real equanimity?"

After the meditation, we had an hour of lively discussion about their experience. Most people reported feeling relaxed. The paramedics, the woman's apparent death, were never mentioned. As a closing for our time together, I spoke about lovingkindness (*metta*) meditation, a practice of wishing well both for oneself and for others. I said that I would say my wishes out loud, and I invited them to recite those same wishes, or similar ones, to themselves silently. I prayed for myself, for my kin, for my friends, for the people in the room, for all beings near and far. In the last moments of our meditating together, I thought again about specifically mentioning the death down the hall. I decided not to. I realized there are always deaths down the hall. The immediate hall, the hall across the street, halls all over the world. Praying for all beings seemed enough.

Several members of the Library Club stayed after the meeting to visit a bit longer, and when I left, parting company with Vivian, the librarian, at the door, I walked down the hall alone past the room where the woman had died. Shades had been pulled down over the window wall, and all I could see as I passed by, in the space at the bottom of the shades, were the feet of a hospital bed, the feet of two chairs drawn close to the bed, and the feet of two men whom I assumed were keeping vigil. I wondered who they were. I knew that the woman who died was, in some way, their person.

Two weeks later, I had a phone call from Tova, my connection to the Library Club, the person who had invited me to the meeting. "I'm tremendously shaken," she said. "You remember Vivian, the librarian? She died yesterday. People do die here every day, like we said, and Vivian had heart disease, so it isn't even surprising, but still . . . She and I were friends." I listened for a long time as Tova told me—stopping from time to time when her voice caught on a sob—why she had loved Vivian and how much she was missing her.

The whole of wisdom is more than the impermanence

of things, more than the truth that the mind by being unwilling to accommodate creates extra pain for itself, more than the fact that things unfold in infinite links of lawful causality. Those very insights, I believe, create the profound awareness that change and loss and sadness and grief are the shared lot of all human beings, and that we are all making our way from one end of life to the other hoping—for whatever intervals of time we can manage it—to feel safe and content and strong and at ease.

The sentence I wish had been added to the mustard seed story is, "And then the Buddha and the woman sat together for a while and cried."

A Little Lower Than the Angels: How Equanimity Supports Kindness

The Buddhist name for the set of four emotional states that includes equanimity and its direct derivatives—impartial goodwill, spontaneous compassion, and genuine appreciation—is *Brahma-Viharas*. A *vihara,* in Pali, the language in which the oldest Buddhist scriptures are written, is a dwelling place. *Brahma* is the word associated with divinity. Classic texts translate the term *Brahma-Viharas* as divine abodes and name the four basic ones: *metta* (friendliness), *karuna* (compassion), *mudita* (empathic joy), and *upekka* (equanimity). I love the term *divine abodes,* and I think of these four states as wonderful conditions of human consciousness in which the mind can rest, feeling at ease, as if at home.

Equanimity, it seems to me, is the ground out of which the other three flavors of benevolent mind arise. Everything depends on it. Equanimity is the capacity of the mind to hold a clear view of whatever is happening, both externally and internally, as well as the ability of the mind to accommodate passion without losing its balance. It's the mind that sees clearly, that meets experience with cordial intent. Because it remains steady, and thus unconfused, it is able to correctly assess the situations it meets. This correct assessment brings with it what the texts call "clear comprehension of purpose," the sure knowledge of what response is required and what is possible. Clear comprehension creates a response, sometimes in action, sometimes just in thought. And because we are humans and have empathy built into our brain structure, when we are touched by what we encounter—and when our minds are balanced—we respond with benevolence. With friendliness or compassion or appreciation. It's a beautiful truth about the potential of human beings. "A little lower than the angels . . ." is the phrase that comes to my mind. Or maybe not lower. Perhaps divine.

Here is how it works. I'll explain it using traditional Buddhist psychology, and I'll include examples of how this works in my life. As you read, see if these centuries-old postulates about the natural responses of the mind are true for you as well.

There are three possible valances of emotional response to every experience: pleasant, unpleasant, and neutral. (Here you might think for a moment about how many times in a day, or even in an hour, you think, "Oh good!" or "Oh phooey!" or even "Boring day. Not much happening.") The Buddha taught that these different flavors of experience are normal, just the facts of life, and that they aren't, by themselves, problematic. They do, however, have the potential to create unhappiness. If they are not recognized, and acknowledged, they create thoughts that carry an imperative for change. "I *need* more of this." "I *must* get rid of this!" "I can't *stand* this." The imperative agitates the mind into confusion.

If, on the other hand, there is enough equanimity in the mind to fend off confusion, wisdom can prevail. Then the mind can respond to ordinary (neutral) situations with goodwill, to frightening (unpleasant) situations with compassion, and to beguiling (pleasant) situations with relaxed, nontroubled appreciation.

Here are three examples that come from my living in France several months each year and traveling back and forth between San Francisco and Paris frequently. The first is about ordinary goodwill, friendliness, which is what the Pali word *metta* means. Perhaps I understate it by calling it ordinary friendliness. It is closer to intentional, omnipresent, devout friendliness based on the awareness that everyone, including oneself—because life is complicated and bodies and minds are often uncomfortable—needs to be working hard all the time just to keep things okay. Here's an example:

The overnight flight from San Francisco to Paris takes more than ten hours, and in the time between midnight and morning, the hours seem longer and the space between the seats in the coach section seems shorter. When I get up to stretch, and perhaps walk down an aisle, I see men and women, old and young, large and small, all unknown to me, some traveling with young children, all trying to figure out how to be comfortable. I see them wrapped up in airplane blankets, scrunched up into whatever position of repose they can organize for themselves, leaning on each other if they are traveling together or trying not to lean on each other if they aren't. Often a man or a woman is patrolling the aisle across from me, holding an infant against his or her chest and moving in the rocking gait that often soothes a baby's distress. I feel a pleasant intimacy with them. I am also trying to stay comfortable. I'm not frightened for them, or for me, because I'm relaxed about flying and I assume we will land successfully, but I wish them well. I enjoy the feeling of my own good-heartedness. In fact, in that moment of mental hand-holding, all those people look a bit more familiar than ordinary strangers. That moment of easy, impartial, benevolent connection—*metta*—buoys up my mind. I feel better as I sit back down in my seat.

Compassion is a variation of *metta*. It's different from relaxed friendliness because it's hard for the mind to stay relaxed and friendly when it encounters a painful, unpleasant situation. In fact, it's normal, and often helpful, for human beings to startle at the awareness of distress. The startle is an instinctive response, a signal to the mind: "Uh-oh. Something is wrong, and you might need to do something." Sometimes, when the startle is strong enough to frighten the mind into confusion, there is a period of unease as the mind tries to cope, either by accommodating the experience or distracting itself if it can't. In contrast, when the mind is able to stay steady, it moves immediately to act, in thought or in deed, in consolation. Traditional Buddhist texts say, "The heart quivers in response."

A man died, suddenly, in the middle of a flight I was on from Paris to San Francisco. I didn't see it happen, but I knew something was wrong because the plane icon on the TV map on the screen in back of the seat in front of mine reversed direction. Soon after that, while the people all around me were showing one another the map and discussing what might be happening, the pilot announced that there had been a medical emergency and requested that any medical personnel come forward to assist. Seymour responded, as he has on previous flights when there has been a call for a physician, and was gone for an hour.

The flight continued as if nothing were awry. Flight attendants served lunch. People watched movies. The icon on the TV turned westward again, and I assumed (correctly, I later learned) that the person had died and that landing for emergency medical care wasn't necessary. I wondered who the person had been, whether he or she had been traveling alone, how his or her family would learn the news. I thought about how my family would feel if it were I, or Seymour, who had died. I thought, "I hope I don't die in a plane," but then I realized that at the center of my startled mind was the awareness that I can't choose when or where I'll die. No one can. Seymour told me later that as the flight personnel carried the dead man's body down the length of the plane to the front galley, where they made the requisite CPR attempts, people turned themselves in their seats and averted their eyes to avoid seeing what was happening. I'm imagining many of those people were thinking, as I was, "That could be me."

I knew that I was too unnerved to read or watch a movie, and I did not want lunch. I sat quietly, and after some few minutes, I heard my mind, on its own, beginning to recite wishes of consolation. "May the dead person's consciousness, wherever it is now, be at ease. May that person's family, on this plane or wherever they are, be strengthened in their loss. May the memory of this person be a blessing to them. May all the people on this plane who have been frightened feel at ease. May I feel at ease. May we land safely." There are traditional Buddhist *karuna* phrases, but I didn't say them. I rarely do because they don't feel natural to me. I make up my own. The traditional ones and the ones I make up mean the same thing: I am aware of painful feelings in me as a result of what is happening to you (or to me), and even though I know that everything passes, now is a suffering time. I hope we all have the strength to endure what is happening without creating extra turmoil. (I don't say all that as a prayer! Much too unwieldy. I say, "May I be at ease" or "May you be at ease" or "May you [I, we, all beings] come to the end of suffering." I say words that are regular speech, like something I might actually say to a person. Saying prayers of consolation always makes me feel better. And it settles my mind. I thought, "This plane is like a small city. Three hundred people. Lots of new babies. Lots of old people. All ages of people in between. People eating, people sleeping, people working, people dreaming. And one person who just died. It's like regular life." I felt sad for the family of the dead person, but I felt okay.

Seymour came back to his seat. He'd spent some time talking with the wife and daughter of the man who died. His death hadn't been a surprise to them. He'd been very ill. Still, it was a shock, happening all of a sudden, in midflight, and among strangers. They seemed to appreciate, he told me, having someone to talk to. We noticed that members of the flight crew took turns sitting with them for the rest of the flight, talking. It might be part of standard airline training, but I think it is, anyway, the instinctive response of human beings to pain. We console. (The heart quivers in response.)

And here's the third story, an example of how the mind (surprisingly) needs equanimity when it meets pleasant situations. It seems as if pleasant situations should leave the mind unruffled. Not true. If an experience inspires yearning, when a moment before, yearning did not exist . . .

On the last day of a winter month spent in France, Seymour and I drove to Les Angles, a ski resort two hours from where we live. We had enjoyed seeing the snow on the peaks of the Pyrenees from our deck, but this was the first time up close. The resort was full of Christmas holiday skiers, and we stood at the bottom of the easiest beginner lift and watched people learning to ski. I was feeling particularly glamorous in my new high-heeled fake-fur-lined boots and purple tweed cap and scarf that my friend Toni had knitted for me. I thought about all the years Seymour and I had skied and all the trails we'd raced each other down before we'd stopped skiing, ten years previously.

"We could ski again," I said. "This is an easy hill. Next year, let's ski."

"No we can't. It's not worth the risk. We're old. We could break something."

"Look, though. This is so easy. It would be such fun to put on skis again. We'd choose a sunny day, like today."

"Forget it. It would be ridiculous. Your back isn't so good. You have bursitis in your shoulder. Last year you pinched a nerve in your neck. Let's go have lunch on the deck. We'll watch the skiing from there."

I caught a glimpse of myself reflected in a window as we walked to the restaurant. I looked shorter and plumper, definitely less glamorous than I had imagined. We ordered lunch. I felt my mind, mired in nostalgia, dragging itself along, seeming to arrive at the table after I did. I thought momentarily of sulking, pretending to be peeved at what I had perceived as a peremptory dismissal. I realized, though, that what I was peeved about was being old. Then I noticed two women sitting at the table adjacent to ours, not unlike me in size and age, carefully made up, coiffed, wearing bright-colored, warm (nonski) jackets and big, beautiful earrings. They were eating hearty lunches, talking and laughing as they ate. I thought they looked marvelous. I looked down at my boots and was glad about the high heels. Later on, before we left, I took some great photos of what I guessed was a three-year-old girl in a pink snowsuit, balanced on her skis with their tips crossed, trying to get her pole straps over her wrists. She looked marvelous, too.

The mind wobbles when it discovers it can't have something it wants, and then, when it catches itself, it appreciates. This wobble was a small one, easily overcome. Other yearnings are much more painful. The cycles, though, of "Oh, a pleasant thing . . . ," "I want it," "I lament not being able to have it. I feel sad," and "This is the way it is. It can't be other, now," are the same regardless of whether the yearning is trivial or tremendous. In the end, relief comes in two stages. The first is the moment that the mind stops struggling and says, "I wanted something different, but this is what I have." The second is the ability to rejoice with other people, delighting in their pleasure. "May you two beautiful women enjoy this lunch and many others." "May you, lovely little girl in pink who reminds me of my own children and grandchildren, grow up to enjoy skiing and also your whole life." (The Pali word for the capacity to fully appreciate and bless is *mudita*.)

And here is one final piece of Buddhist theory that I can add, now that I've told these three stories of what seem to me to be the natural goodwill responses of the mind balanced by wisdom. The responses of friendliness, compassion, and appreciation that I felt in these three situations—all situational permutations of basic goodwill—depended on my mind's being relaxed and alert enough to notice both what was happening around me and what was happening as my internal response. In each case, even though the situation included challenge, my mind had enough equanimity in it to allow me to stay connected with affection. My refuge was my own good nature, available for expression.

And it might have been otherwise. If my mind, in the long overnight flight, had been preoccupied with stories of my life, past or anticipated, or had it been agitated by fears about flying, or even if I had simply been too tired to pay attention to the scene around me, I would have missed it. I would not have been able to recognize the fundamental truth about human beings—that we do our best to keep ourselves comfortable, in orderly ways so as not to disturb others, in whatever situations we find ourselves—and I would have missed the opportunity to be touched by human courage. Instead of feeling warmly connected to the other people on my flight, I would have been indifferent. On the outside, I would have looked the same. On the inside, I would not have felt nearly as good.

And I really don't know if my mind could have stayed balanced enough to rest in consolation if someone had taken ill, or died, in the row next to mine. I might have felt frightened about not having the skills to help. I've been with friends as they died, but I wanted to be there, and I wasn't surprised. Perhaps, on a plane and caught off guard, I'd be wishing that it weren't happening or that I were somewhere else. I don't know. If my mind was overwhelmed by resentment or fear, the wisdom that reminds me that these things happen—people take ill, and die, according to conditions beyond their control, just as I will someday—would not have been available to comfort me. I might have forgotten to pray.

And perhaps if I had been less happy than I was on the day at Les Angles, I would have fallen prey to envy or jealousy, and to avoid recognizing those feelings, I might have started a quarrel about being spoken to peremptorily. As it turned out, I had enough wisdom available to me to think, "Things change. That was then. Now is now. There are other pleasures I can enjoy. Everyone takes turns being able to do this or that in life. We can for a while, and then we can't. May everyone, including me, enjoy this moment."

Indifference, pity, envy, and jealousy are what the Buddha called the "near enemies of the *Brahma-Viharas*." Indifference, for example, might masquerade as equanimity, looking very balanced and even, but representing, in fact, the very opposite of emotional connection. (Think of the expression "I couldn't care less," which I've always heard as having a sad ring to it.) Pity looks a little like compassion, because it acknowledges suffering, but it is still an arm's-length awareness of the pain and carries some aversion in it. "It's too bad this is happening to you," the mind thinks, without remembering "This, or some other painful thing, will sometime happen to me or my kin. May all beings always be comforted in their suffering." And without balancing awareness in the mind, delight and affection morph into envy and jealousy when other people's joys are joys we covet or when we require something in return for our friendship. All of the near enemies are unhappy, tense states. The *Brahma-Viharas* all establish connections that nourish and enliven the moment. The near enemies create distance and isolation.

Wishing others well in moments of good fortune, wishing them well when they are struggling, and acting with ordinary benevolence as people are going about the regular business of life—appreciation, consolation, and friendliness—keeps me connected to the world outside of myself as well as to my own natural goodness. Both those perspectives act for me as safety nets. Staying alertly connected to the world outside myself keeps me from falling into the limitations of self-absorption from which no reality check into wisdom is possible. And the reconnection with my own benevolent nature, each time it happens, protects me from the despair of feeling that nothing I (or anyone else) could do can make a difference. Safely connected to my life, and reassured of my essential goodness, I feel at ease, at home, really in the most sublime of homes.

And here's one more detail from the traditional accounts of the Buddha's enlightenment experience that—because the Buddha sounds so human in it—is particularly inspiring to me. He is reported to have hesitated before starting out to teach, thinking of the enormity of the task before him. Some legends say that heavenly messengers appeared to him urging him on, reminding him of what benefit his news about ending suffering would be to those people who heard it. The Buddha's decision to teach was, presumably, the result of hearing those heavenly messengers.

I know that in situations where I am hesitating about doing something—something I know will be helpful—my own kindness pushes me to do it. I anticipate how bad I'll feel if I don't act. I think it was the same for the Buddha. "Heavenly messengers," I think, are our impulses of natural kindness.

We Are All Imperiled:
How Kindness Restores Equanimity

So far, we've seen how establishing equanimity in the mind creates the conditions for the arising of the profound wisdom that in turn promotes kindness as the natural empathic response. The converse is also true. The expression of kindness establishes equanimity that in turn sustains wisdom—which is always consoling.

My friend and teaching colleague Tamara phoned unexpectedly one afternoon with the news, "I'm just calling to say that you don't need to worry about me." Tamara had undergone surgery for suspected ovarian cancer just a few weeks previously, and the original pathology report had been negative. A week later, with more experts reviewing the data, the diagnosis was changed to early-stage cancer, and she had her first chemotherapy treatment. When I heard the excited "no need to worry" message, I had the instant thought, "Praise be! They've reviewed the pathology again and she doesn't have cancer." "I will be safe," Tamara continued, "even though Hurricane Frances is coming right toward Palm Beach. Some friends who have a house with fewer windows, one less isolated and exposed than mine, have invited me to sit out the storm with them. So I'm leaving home, and you won't find me here if you call. Just know I am safe!"

I checked the progress of Hurricane Frances on The Weather Channel for the next three days and thought about how, because I had someone especially dear to me in the middle of it, the storm had become important to me. The meteorologists standing in the rain, clutching their Windbreaker collars up around their necks with one hand and holding a microphone in the other, shouting over noisy winds to describe conditions and update evacuation instructions, became familiar to me. One young newscaster ducked suddenly out of camera range to avoid some flying roof tiles coming her way and then scrambled back up to finish her report. I admired her courage. I found myself wondering if her mother was watching her on TV.

After the storm, Tamara phoned and described her experience: "The storm wall came through in the middle of the night. It made a tremendous noise, like a freight train. The windows rattled. The power was out, so we had no news and no light. My friends and I sat on the living room sofa, by candlelight, huddled together in our pajamas and robes. We mostly sat quietly, but whenever it became most fearsome, we prayed. We prayed that we would be safe and well and also that everyone else around us in the storm would be, too."

I told Tamara about the brief moment in which I had imagined she didn't have cancer. She said, "You know, I didn't think about the cancer while all of this was happening. I didn't forget that I have it. It just wasn't what mattered." She laughed and added, "This would be a great title for a talk: 'Worrying Is Futile: You Don't Know What to Worry About First.' And anyway, during the storm, everyone was imperiled, cancer or no cancer."

Before we ended that conversation, Tamara said, "Really what I learned is that when I realize I have no control over a situation—like with the hurricane, and maybe the cancer— being with friends who love me, whom I love, makes it okay. And that praying for everyone around me when I was most frightened got me through the worst times."

WISE EFFORT

Just Do It: Wise Effort as Wisdom Practice

Wise Effort, deliberately choosing to shift the mind's attention so that equanimity can reestablish itself, is a different route to wisdom than practicing mindfulness or applying concentration, but its goal is the same. Mindfulness restores balance, and elicits wisdom, by noticing and identifying experiences in the mind and recognizing the patterns that emerge. It understands confusing energies as being transient and insubstantial, and often can maintain the mind's basic clarity even in their presence. Concentration restores the mind to balance by providing the direct antidotes to confusing energies in the mind so that wisdom is revealed. Wise Effort sounds to me in its classical definition, and feels to me when I can do it, like a determined leap over intermediary steps to the desired end point. I think of it often in the words of the advertisement for Nike running shoes, "Just do it."

Although I want to tell you that "just doing it" isn't always easy, I found myself, not long ago, in the middle of walking up the hill at Spirit Rock Meditation Center from the dining room to the meditation hall, singing to myself (quietly, of course) the lyrics to a popular tune of the nineteen forties. When I listened to the words, I laughed. "Thirty years of practice," I thought, "and the lofty has been replaced by the banal. Has it all come to this?" What I heard myself singing begins with the line "Look for the silver lining when e'er a cloud appears in the blue." Do you remember it? It goes on to say that "somewhere, the sun is shining," followed by the encouraging reminder, "And so the right thing to do is make it shine for you."

I dismissed my mind's impulse to continue its attempt at comic teasing—"What's next? Lemons into lemonade?"—because I soon realized two things. The first is how relentlessly my mind tries to be clever, even if it is at my own expense, and how trivializing and tedious that suddenly felt. The second was that the lyrics aren't banal. Saying that somewhere the sun is shining is an innovative way to say that things pass, that the current difficulty won't last. Saying that you can make the sun shine for you, produce a happier circumstance for yourself, is—in addition to being an inspiring statement of faith—a good way to describe the role of intention. I often describe my own spiritual practice as an ongoing attempt "to keep my head screwed on straight" or "to think outside the box" about whatever challenge has just upset me. Perhaps a more elegant way to say that would be, "My practice is remembering that although whatever is happening, including my emotional response to it, is the lawful consequence of myriad causes that are beyond my control, the relationship I hold toward it all is within my control. I can choose on behalf of happiness."

That's a radical thought, but the Buddha was a radical psychologist. The verse that meditators are instructed to repeat to themselves in order to consolidate their equanimity is, "All individuals are heirs to their own karma. Their happiness [or, I am adding, my own happiness] depends on their actions, not on my wishes for them." Heir to your own karma doesn't mean "You get what you deserve." I think it means "You get what you get." Bad things happen to good people. My happiness depending on my action means, to me, that it depends on my action of choosing compassion— for myself as well as for everyone else—rather than contention.

A standard textbook rendering of the Buddha's teaching

of Wise Effort always has four parts: (1) Notice the presence in the mind of wholesome states (peace or happiness or any of the *Brahma-Viharas*) and maintain them. (2) Notice the absence in the mind of wholesome states and cultivate them. (3) Notice the absence of unwholesome states in the mind (anger, greed, resentment) and keep them out. (4) Notice the presence in the mind of unwholesome states and eliminate them. In one particularly fiery sermon, the Buddha suggests a variety of ways to rid the mind of entrenched painful thoughts that are generating unwholesome feelings, and he ends by instructing meditators—when all else fails—to clench their teeth together and, with all their strength, will away such thoughts and feelings. I like that.

All the other suggestions in that sermon, up to the final "Get a grip" directive, are instructions for reframing the story surrounding the painful experience so that one's own mind does not feel victimized. Here's a contemporary example:

My friend Susan was standing knee-high in the ocean on what seemed like a calm surf day in Zihuatanejo, Mexico, when a wave picked her up and dropped her over onto her ankle in a way that caused it to break in several places. Susan knew she was in trouble. The pain was severe. She was alone and no one was nearby. She sat up, legs stretched out toward the sea, and let the next several waves carry her

back onto the shore. Then she waved and shouted until people noticed her and carried her out of the water and onto a
chaise longue in the shade of a beach umbrella. Someone
called the paramedics.

It was the fifth day of a seven-day yoga and meditation
retreat, a day in which participants had been invited to
spend the time outside of structured meetings in silence and
solitude. Moments after Susan's rescue, though, word of her
accident spread down the beach, and other retreatants,
some of them her professional colleagues, some still newly
familiar strangers, rushed to her aid. Someone put a wet
cloth on her brow. Someone else improvised an ice pack out
of a plastic bag and ice cubes from the cold drink conces-
sion. Someone said, "Take a deep breath. Now another
breath. You'll be fine. Help is on the way."

Susan said, "I'm so sorry to cause all this fuss. This was
supposed to be a quiet day."

"Don't even think about that."

"It's fine."

"The important thing is for you to get taken care of."

"I'll get you water to sip."

"I'll cover you with a towel."

The paramedics arrived, and because the beach was lo-
cated several flights of narrow stone steps down from the
road, Susan's transfer to the ambulance required her being

strapped into a stretcher and being carried, one person in front and one in back, up the stairs. Several of us in attendance followed close behind and watched the stretcher being maneuvered to make the required turns. I sat with Susan in the ambulance as the paramedics prepared to leave with her. The topic of that morning's meditation class had been the possibility of framing a difficult experience in a context large enough to maintain equanimity in the mind. Susan looked over at me and smiled.

"This is the best first experience I ever had of needing to be rescued by a paramedic," she said. We both laughed.

"I'll tell the group you said that when I am teaching tonight," I said. "They'll like that."

The group did like it. They applauded. It buoys up everyone's courage to be reminded that there is a redemptive perspective, a wider "frame" that the mind can put around an event to make it—at least temporarily—more manageable. In truth, although the moment in the ambulance was lightened, there were many difficult times for Susan over the months it took for her to recuperate from surgery. The fact that the redeemed moments are temporary—well, everything is temporary! The fact that they can happen—in a moment of gratitude, of appreciation, of anything—is what matters. They give the mind a chance to relax, to regain its natural capacity for being a repository of wisdom—in this case, of the specific wisdom that this situation of difficulty, although uncomfortable, is time-limited. The awareness "This hurts a lot" and "Tomorrow's trip back to New York City is likely to be very hard" can exist alongside—and be modified by—all the other truths: This will pass. People are kind. Even strangers are aroused by someone else's trouble and are moved to offer help. Being alive is a mysterious and precarious thing. That life is happening at all—however it is happening—is a miracle. You really never know what the next minute is going to bring, so living fully in this moment is the only constantly reappearing option for happiness.

Omitting None: *Metta* Practice as Wise Effort

I'm quite surprised to find myself introducing *metta* practice as Wise Effort practice. I learned it as a concentration practice—reciting, continuously and silently to myself, *metta* blessing phrases—and it's still an important practice for me. I've also long thought of *metta* as the spontaneous response to mindfulness, the natural benevolence that arises in moments of clear connection. Nevertheless, as this book has unfolded, it has become ever more clear to me that the steadfast decision to cultivate a noncontentious mind, one that meets experience without the imperative that it be different, requires ongoing, unflagging effort. It is the continuing attempt to cultivate a mind filled—according to the *Metta Sutta* (Sermon on Lovingkindness)—with enough "gladness and safety" to be able to wish, without exception, "May all beings be at ease."

According to legend, the Buddha taught *metta*—resolute well-wishing for oneself as well as others—as a protection practice for monks who were about to go off on their own to meditate in jungles, apart from the community, in situations where they might be frightened. The traditional list of practice benefits includes immunity to "poisons and weapons and fire." For me, having my mind in a benevolent mood so I am protected from animosity, resentment, jealousy, or envy—from the pain of feeling disconnected from others—is the immunity I want. In fact, although an important *metta* chant begins with the words "May I be free of enmity and danger," which I imagine was originally meant as "danger from external sources," I always think, "free of enmity in me."

The technique of formal practice begins with blessings for oneself and ends with blessings for everything alive. One particular phrase in the *Metta Sutta,* the two words "omitting none," seems to me the essential key to the entire teaching. Peace of mind, I take it to mean, depends on unconditional benevolence. In other words, any antipathy in the mind at all, any contention, obviates personal happiness. With happiness as the goal, the technique of systematically blessing everyone the mind can think of routs out hidden aversion and any leftover clinging to grudges. (I sometimes say, at this point in describing *metta* practice, that it sounds as if I am taking my mind to the laundry. In fact, it feels that way.) What inspires my determination to discover and resolve any hidden animosity in me is my awareness that no matter whom I am thinking of, I myself am always the principal beneficiary of my benevolence. Having my mind in unrestricted caring mode means that my prayers have *already* been answered. It means that I am free of the suffering of enmity and the danger of remaining unhappy. It means I am fully connected, alive.

I think the psychology of the formal *metta* practice design is brilliant. It works two ways. First of all, the repetition of blessings soothes the tension in a mind clouded by distaste. The kind thoughts that fill the mind cause it, at least for the time it's busy blessing, to stop telling itself inflammatory stories such as "He wronged me" or "She abused me." We can't bless and simultaneously be imagining retribution and revenge. It would be like trying to drive your car in "Drive" and "Reverse" at the same time. It doesn't work.

When the stories fueling the upset mind stop, the mind gets a chance to relax. At this point, it can accommodate new information.

This new information—and there are two predictable varieties of it—further neutralizes any leftover disagreeable feelings. First to arrive is the more comprehensive view about anyone that arises in the mind when it relaxes enough to stop fixating on one particular difficulty. "Well, they *did* do this, but in other situations . . ." Or "I guess he doesn't *always* do this. . . ." Tense minds think in terms of "always" and "never" as a quick summary opinion. Minds with equanimity in them think, "This" and "Also, this."

The second variety of new information comes from following a particular instruction in formal *metta* texts. The instruction is, "Think about what's good about this person," as someone arrives, in person or in thought. This, by the way, was the clue that first caused me to think of *metta* practice as Wise Effort. Thinking of something good can be problematic.

It isn't hard to do, of course, when someone you normally love has annoyed you. There are probably many choices of "good" things. "He brings me coffee in bed in the morning." "She is so sweet to my elderly father." "Endlessly loyal to worthy causes." The mind "smiles" when it thinks any of those thoughts, and it relaxes. In a more expansive, relaxed state, it remembers, "I am offended now, but really, it's just that I'm startled. We really do love each other. May we both be well."

It's also not hard to think complimentary thoughts about people toward whom I feel reasonably neutral. Whenever the shopkeeper in my small town who is always helpful and polite startles me by offering, unsolicited, a political opinion completely at odds with mine, I am glad, even eager, to thank him for helping me shop. If I do, I can get in my car and remember his kindness and not replay the story that begins, "It's people with views like his . . ." If my mind can refrain from vilifying him—which isn't hard to do because, after all, why upset myself?—I can continue to feel friendly. Whatever his politics, he is well mannered and I like doing business there.

By now, I'm sure you've figured out what effortful practice will be. Indeed, when I teach *metta,* people often stop me at this point and ask, "Surely you aren't going to expect me to bless . . . ?" and name some generally agreed upon badly thought of person. I go on to say that traditional texts call this person "the enemy," and I agree that it is difficult— very difficult—to conjure up some mitigating laudable thing to think about a person whose very name evokes aversion. Indeed, when my colleagues and I teach *metta,* we normally encourage people to begin with blessings for themselves, well-beloved friends, and familiar strangers (neighbors, mail deliverers) before "taking on" people who evoke aversion. And in deference to contemporary mores, we often use the term *difficult person* rather than *enemy* when we introduce this part of practice. Still, the mind balks at the instruction "Think of the good about this person."

"Are you kidding? Never! That would be giving in. Making that person okay."

Of course it isn't making the person okay at all. It is making your own mind, startled into defensiveness by the thought of the terribleness of the other person, okay. Okay enough to relax. There is always more in anyone's life than the particular thing he or she did (or is doing) that offends me. By remembering something—"He raised two sons alone"; "She would have been a wonderful singer had her family been able to afford training for her"; or even "This political leader whose policies I dislike probably believes he is right, just as I believe I am"—I can change someone from a monolithic representation of pain to a human being with whom I have at least one thing in common: we are both doing the best we can.

When I can do that, it is I who am immediately better off.

I can seriously dislike people, or not like what they do,

and still not make them my enemies. Wishing people well means I've stopped being afraid of them, stopped holding them, metaphorically speaking, at emotional arm's length. Relieved of the sense of needing to be on the defensive— after all, I am rarely in danger, even in person, with people I don't like and never in danger in thought—I am changed. Most of the time, I do not start liking people I didn't previously admire. Even if I realize that they are suffering and that they couldn't be different, I still don't like them. What changes for me when my mind drops its aversion is that I realize—because I keep forgetting and need to remember again and again—that forgiveness and goodwill are my most reliable refuge.

Here are the two formulas that I use for formal *metta* practice:

May I be free of enmity and danger.
May I have mental happiness.
May I have physical happiness.
May I have ease of well-being.

And,

May I feel contented and safe.
May I feel protected and pleased.
May my physical body support me with strength.
May my life unfold smoothly with ease.

I learned the first set of phrases from my teacher, Sharon Salzberg, more than twenty years ago, and I said them so much that they are still what comes to my mind naturally if I am startled, as I sometimes am by sudden bumps in an otherwise smooth plane flight. Perhaps they'll stay in my mind the longest as I get older, just as it often happens that elderly people revert to their native language. That's fine with me, because I like those phrases, and I have a tune I sing them to.

The second set of phrases are ones I created and learned to say for my own *metta* practice in response to requests from students for more contemporary words to say. Both sets of phrases carry the same wishes for safety, contentment, vigor, and ease. I have tunes for these phrases as well.

Here's a practice idea for right now. Choose one of those sets of phrases. (Later on, if you want others, you'll make up your own. Just for now, as an experiment, choose one set.) Plan on taking some time to say those words over and over, as you would an ardent prayer. Set some time aside for this. (Fifteen minutes would be a good start.) Then sit comfortably. Later on, you can say these phrases walking about or doing chores or even riding your bike—but for now, just sit. That way you can look at the words.

Say each phrase as if you expect it will feel different in your mind—they are slightly different wishes—and feel how each of them echoes in your mind and body. You can say them in the "May I . . ." form in which they are written or "May you . . . ," thinking of a well-beloved person, if you prefer. In either case, you can feel the wishes in your body. Later on, you can try saying blessings for other people. For now, keep it simple. And don't evaluate your experience. You can't be doing it wrong. Just say a phrase, pause to feel it in your mind and body, and then say the next one. Remember, it is meant to be effortful—you are vigorously eliminating any bitterness in your mind by sweetening it with blessings—so stay with the phrases even if your attention tires. The important thing is to stay with the same phrases and say them over and over. And remember, it's not the phrases that make the difference. It's your resolve, your own intention to have your mind rest in its own goodness, that makes the difference. You are reminding your mind, diligently, to care—which is what it does naturally.

Keeping the Mind Hospitable:
Wise Speech as Wise Effort

When, more than twenty years ago, Seymour and I met the family of the woman our son Peter planned to marry, we knew he was in good hands when we heard the speech patterns of the bride's mother. "Here comes my son Jorge," she would say, "who is such a dear man, such a wonderful, poetic soul." And "Here comes my daughter Natalia. You'll love her, I'm sure." And "Here comes my sister-in-law. She is sometimes a bit harsh, but really, she has had a hard life." Everyone arrived with a story that was, if not flattering, at least forgiving. I thought of Noemi's practice then—as I do now—as keeping her mind hospitable. It's effortful practice, of course, because one needs to be doing it all the time—every moment of experience arrives with an editorial decision: "I like it" or "I don't like it"—but it is also immediately rewarding. Speech that compliments is, by definition, free from derision, which clouds the mind with enemies and makes it tense. Kind speech makes the mind feel safe and also glad.

This is one of those points at which separate elements of the Buddha's Eightfold Path of practice conflate into one another. Wise Speech—one of the triad of morality trainings that, traditionally, begins the path—is usually explained in terms of speech that is addressed to others. It mandates speech that is true and kind and helpful and timely and gentle. In terms of Wise Effort, I think of training my mind so that the inner narrative that accompanies me as I go about my days is true and kind and helpful and timely and gentle.

Since that narrative is often a spontaneous editorial opinion of how I'm doing, I'd like it to be, if not flattering, at least forgiving. (It would mean, if I could manage it, that I had stayed balanced enough to remain wise: I am, after all, always doing the best I can.)

Who knows how many voices have gone into shaping my inner narrative? My parents, my teachers, the culture, I suppose everything with a view as to what is good and what isn't. Sometimes, if I catch my mind in the middle of making up a demoralizing opinion of me, I can hear my mind correct itself: "That's not true!" A friend of mine once taught me to say, when I identified a voice from the past shaping my mind in the present moment, "Thanks, Mom," or "Thanks, whomever," as a way of distancing myself from an unskillful identification without blaming anyone. Maybe a good way to think about this all is as teaching the mind to have good manners, to be hospitable. My favorite translation of the Pali word *metta* is friendliness. If my mind stays in a friendly mood, I am happy.

My grandfather's speech practice—he never missed doing it, so I count it as a practice although he probably didn't think of it that way—was definitely shaped by his cultural background as an Eastern European Jew. I like to think it was shaped by his good nature as well. Whenever he spoke, he added one of two specific modifying clauses, protection blessings, after the name of each person whom he mentioned. For example, he might have said, "My daughter Gladys, may she rest in peace, had a more relaxed nature than my daughter Miriam, may she live and be well." He did it with all names, and in both neutral and difficult situations. He could have said, "My grandson Henry, may he live and be well, is a very good cook." Of a long-ago disappointment, he said, "My uncle Jacob, may he rest in peace, who I was depending on to help me when I came to America, couldn't do it, so I was on my own." About his difficulties with his third wife (he'd outlived two others), he said, "Bessie, may she live and be well, has become too cranky to live with these days . . ." as an explanation of why he had left her, and his home, and come to live with me.

What seems clear to me now, in retrospect, is that my grandfather's protection blessings—including, as they did, people who had offended him—protected him from having any negative opinions turn accidentally into ill will. He could tell his life story without vilifying anyone. Not long before he died, a year before his hundredth birthday, he told me, with certainty and with obvious pleasure, "After I'm gone, there will be no one who will say a bad thing about me." He had never allowed his mind to create or harbor enemies.

Familiar Strangers: Intentional Appreciation Practice

If ever I have a moment of "stage fright"—it happens sometimes just before I start to teach a large audience in a city far from home—I look out at the group and think, first of all, "I love you." I really do. It's a shorthand reminder to myself that everyone who has come is planning to enjoy hearing what I say. They have not come as critics. They've come as friends. They are "on my side." I look at the people in front of me as if I expect to recognize someone—and, in fact, everyone looks like somebody. As soon as I smile, people smile back, and my sense of "Uh-oh, I don't know anyone here" changes to "We are familiar strangers." Then I relax, start to tell a story, and feel quite at home.

Of course, the easiest teaching situations are ones in which I don't need to remind myself that people will be glad to hear me because the community itself reminds me. The Kripalu Center for Yoga & Health, in Lenox, Massachusetts, where I've been a guest teacher for more than a decade, does appreciation as a spiritual practice. The program brochure doesn't say that—yoga classes and psychology seminars are the listed offerings—but you feel a definite texture of goodwill in the air as soon as you arrive there.

When I took my daughter Emily with me to Kripalu for her first visit—I was to be a speaker at a conference there on yoga and Buddhism—she could feel the communal good mood immediately. "Something magic is going on here," she said. "People are incredibly nice to each other." Our hypothesis was that the yoga and the meditation—there were practice sessions all day between the conference program presentations, and Emily and I did them together—relaxed everyone's mind so that natural appreciation, everyone thanking at every opportunity, participants as well as presenters, took over. "Thank you for that class." "Thank you for being such attentive participants." "Thank you." "Thank you."

Also, every conference speaker was introduced with abundant praise for his or her talents, and each presentation was followed with immediate praise for its most outstanding points. After I spoke, Emily asked, "Did you get nervous, Mom, with so many people there? You didn't sound like it. You looked like you were having a really good time."

"I was having a great time," I replied. "By the time Kavi finished introducing me, I was so pleased by the great things he said about me, I felt like I couldn't make a mistake. I was thrilled to be teaching, and I think I taught better than I ever have. It never occurred to me that I should worry."

I think our hypothesis that it was the yoga and meditation that had made everyone relaxed and appreciative was certainly a part of the sense of delighted friendliness that filled the hallways, even the elevators. What I also think, now, is that the escalating communal good mood was more than gratitude for all the program offerings, wonderful as they were. I think it was gratitude for being able to feel safe, to know that no display of hostility in any form could possibly happen. When I am privy to disparaging critiques, even when they are not directed at me, I feel unnerved and my mind is roused into protective mode. I think of it as a basic survival response, and I'm glad I have it so I can run away from real danger. But it's fatiguing to live *en garde*. A week of communal safety from rebuke or challenge was amazing.

On Sunday midday, as the conference ended, there was a flurry of photo taking, phone-number exchanges, and hugs all around. I hugged all my colleagues, and Emmy did as well. Folks I did not know who wanted to say "Thank you" or wanted to say "It was fun being on the yoga mat next to you" waited their turn to say whatever they said, and they hugged me. If Emmy was standing nearby, they often said, "It was great seeing you and your mom having such a good time together," and hugged her as well. The Kripalu driver who took us to the Hartford airport ended his curbside goodbyes with hugs for us both and said, "You were both terrific! Come back soon!"

The last piece of our trip home, after the coast-to-coast flight, was an hour on the airport bus. Emily and I were the last people off the bus, and by the time I paid the fare collector at the exit, everyone else had already claimed their luggage and left. The driver was waiting with our two bags at the rear of the bus, and as we hurried to pick them up, I looked over at Emmy, who, at that moment, looked at me. We both realized that we had each been dead on course to hug him.

We didn't. We said, "Thank you very much," and took our suitcases, hurried away, and burst out laughing.

"You were going to hug the bus driver!"

"You were, too! I saw you headed directly toward him!"

"I was."

"It's hysterical," Emily said. "We've caught a hugging virus."

I think I enjoy retelling this story as much as I do because the hugging image is such a literal representation of the "heartfelt embrace" we feel in the company of people with whom we feel safe. Hugging is the opposite of "giving the cold shoulder" or "holding at arm's length." What I really hope we caught is an appreciative virus. Or maybe it would be better to call it the appreciative vaccine, since it keeps the mind immune to enmity.

I wonder if the bus driver knew that we intended to hug him. I hope he did.

Sweetening the Mind:
Wise Effort as Clear Discernment

One of my friends and teachers, Reb Zalman Schachter-Shalomi, told me years ago, "The mind is like tofu. By itself, it has no taste. Everything depends on the flavor of the marinade it steeps in." I've used his tofu-mind analogy a lot. If I am entertaining irritating opinions—"This is no good." "This shouldn't be happening"—I'll see my mind tumble into despair or get suddenly enraged over a relatively minor stimulus. I can even see it "enjoying" staying embittered, as if it gets pleasure from making a case for itself about how bad it feels. I can even sometimes see it waver when the opportunity to sweeten the marinade arises. It seems like a ridiculous debate—Happiness? Unhappiness?—but I also can figure out the possible reasons for the waver.

Here's a story. It's ordinary. It comes from my life, but maybe you'll recognize yourself in it. Change a few of the minor details, and it becomes anyone's story.

I got a $270 ticket for driving alone in the car-pool lane on a drizzly February afternoon. I was already exhausted, and the ticket felt like the latest annoying episode in a day that had already seemed full of annoyances.

"Officer," I said, "please listen to me. I did not do that purposely. My daughter called me on my car phone. She was distraught. She needed to talk. I was trying to listen to her and still drive carefully, and I had just said, 'Hey! I see I am accidentally in the car-pool lane. I need to get back into the traffic. I have to hang up' when I saw your lights flashing. Please, please, *please* do not give me a ticket."

He said, "I need to see your driver's license and your car registration." I watched him in my rearview mirror as he went back to his motorcycle and made a phone call.

"Good, " I thought. "He'll see I've got a clean record, and he'll let me off."

He came back and gave me a ticket. "It's not a moving violation," he said. "It's just a fine. Drive carefully as you get back into the traffic."

As I drove off, I saw him getting back on his motorcycle. "Where were you," I thought, "ten minutes ago when that little green Corvette doing eighty miles an hour was weaving back and forth across all the lanes and menacing lives?" I was mad.

The phone rang again. Same daughter. "What happened?"

"I got a ticket."

"I'm so upset. It's my fault."

"Don't be upset," I said. "What happened happened. Getting upset is extra. I'll just be more vigilant from now on about where the car-pool lane is. I'll learn from it. I'll call you later."

Off the phone, free from the constraints of appropriate behavior, my irritated mind went looking for more griev-ances to stew over. "If only that meeting at Spirit Rock hadn't gone on so late," I thought, choosing the next-to-last annoyance to focus on. "I can't believe how some people be-labor a point so endlessly. If we had finished on time, there wouldn't have been so much traffic. And the car-pool lane hours wouldn't have started."

The last miles of my drive home are off the highway, and most of them are a country road that winds through vine-yards. Usually I enjoy that part of the drive, but I was dis-tressed, eager to get home. I could hear my mind organizing the litany of indignant woe that I planned to recite as soon as I got in the door. I tried out several opening lines: "You can't imagine the totally terrible day I had. . . ." "Car phones are a menace. . . ." "Where are the cops when you need them?"

Just then, turning a corner, I startled a jackrabbit cross-ing the middle of the road. I braked hard and skidded for-ward. The jackrabbit took off and sailed in an impossibly high arc over the path of my oncoming car, landed in the grassy hill at the side of the road, and hopped out of sight. My heart jumped as well, first in alarm, then in relief at not having hit the jackrabbit, then in delight at its magically graceful, lifesaving leap.

As I drove on, I watched my mind debating between reviving the woes of the day story or switching to the amazing jackrabbit story. The complaining seemed "juicier." I remembered that I'd once learned that the conventional wisdom for TV news broadcasts is "Lead with trouble. It captures the attention." Then I realized that the woe presentation I'd been preparing had been an attempt to deflect Seymour's attention from the traffic ticket and avoid possible criticism.

"You got a *what*??? Doesn't seem very mindful to me. Do you know how much that fine is?"

Driving up the hill to my house, I realized that my irritable thought tirade was also deflecting my attention from the fact that I was tired and hungry and ashamed of myself for getting a ticket. So I arrived home and told the story straight: "I just saw a phenomenal jackrabbit. I am tired and hungry. And I got a $270 ticket for driving alone in the carpool lane. I feel bad about it. I wish I'd been paying better attention. Let's fix dinner."

The jackrabbit story is an example of a relatively easy loosening of the grip of an afflictive emotion on the entire territory of the mind. Even though I was tired and hungry and remorseful and embarrassed about getting the ticket, I was still able to notice the escape route that the jackrabbit—and its miraculous leap—offered me, and I could let it into my mind along with the traffic ticket, the long meeting, my fatigue, and my hunger. Once I did that, I had a clearer view of what was feeding my story and perpetuating my distress. Knowing more always leads to better decisions.

And it would have been different if any part of the story were different: If the ticket had been more expensive. If I'd still been miles from home. If—and I am so glad this did not happen—I'd hit the jackrabbit. And if I hadn't been sure, in my heart of hearts, that Seymour would tease me but he wouldn't scold. But things were the way they were, not different, and so my mind could—in a moment, so it qualifies as right effort but seemed actually effortless—readjust itself back into balance, and wisdom. The whole thing wasn't a big deal—just an evening rescued from turmoil so that two old friends could have dinner together—but it seemed to me like grace.

A Break in the Clouds: Opportunities for Wise Effort

I recall how happy I felt the first time I realized that I could say "Enough! No more of this for now!" to a suffering mind state. I'd previously believed that I was destined to struggle with unhappy states until they ran their course like bouts of the flu. In my daily life, and especially on retreat, where there is nothing to do other than listen to my mind, I often thought, "I hope I don't accidentally think about . . ." or "May I just not remember. . . . ," lest uncomfortable feelings take over my mind as fevers take over my body when I am ill. It's hard to be hiding from thoughts on retreat and it's hard to be hiding from them in life. So it was a relief to discover that I didn't need to. I realized that I could remember whatever I remembered without disregarding or suppressing or repressing the feelings the memories brought with them, and when it was too much, I could—at the very least—take a break.

My discovery happened at the end of a retreat day, not long after I'd begun my meditation practice. I had left the last afternoon session in tears. Earlier that morning, I'd remembered—out of the blue, it had seemed—a painful event of my childhood, and I'd felt the distress in my mind and body associated with that experience as if it were new. That memory then seemed to dislodge a whole stream of associated memories. As the day progressed, I felt as if I had accidentally wandered into a movie theater showing a retrospective, "All the Terrible Times in Sylvia's Life When She Has Felt Just Like This." I once heard the psychologist

Stanislaus Grof describing the mind as if it were a box of bobbins of threads in a variety of colors such as one might store in the drawer of a sewing machine. New experiences, he explained, would get "wound onto" the bobbin that held the same emotional charge, triggering the recall of old memories. I have "bobbins" of "times I have felt embarrassed," "times I have felt furious," "times I have felt abandoned." I also have "bobbins" of epiphany moments, "times I have felt, 'For this very moment, life has been worth living,' " but they do not seem to appear as spontaneously. The "uncomfortable bobbins" carrying chronological histories of similarly charged difficult emotional experiences seem all too eager to reveal themselves.

I don't remember the particular set of disturbing memories of that retreat day long ago, but I remember that as the day progressed, I became sadder and sadder, more and more demoralized by my inability to "pull myself together," and increasingly distraught about what to do next.

I decided to take a shower. Probably I thought that if I refreshed my body, my mind might feel better and the fog of gloom that seemed to surround me might dissipate. I started down the road that led from the meditation hall to the small cabin a quarter of a mile away that I was sharing with three other women. Just then, the bell announcing afternoon tea sounded. My mind paused long enough in its narrative of "I'll get to the cabin. I'll shower. Maybe I'll feel better" to make the thought "I wonder if there will be cookies for tea?"

I noticed that thought. It's important for me to tell you that I don't normally eat cookies or, indeed, anything very sweet. I've never had a taste for sweets. The "cookies for tea" thought did not inspire lust. It was simply a thought, a moment of neutral interest—sometimes there were cookies, sometimes not—and my mind simply wondered. What I specifically noticed was that in the moment of neutral, alert wondering, there was no sadness. I was excited. I felt as if my mind had paused in its downward journey like an elevator that unexpectedly stops at a floor whose button you did not push. The story I had been telling myself, "I am surrounded by impermeable gloom," had changed to "There is a break in the clouds." I turned back toward the dining room.

Drinking my tea—without cookies—I was both relieved by the new energy I felt and amused by the meteorological metaphor I'd chosen. I explain it to people now by reminding them of the situation at Cape Canaveral when a space shuttle is poised for launch at eighteen seconds and counting and the clock is stopped because the sky fills with clouds. Television commentators covering the flight keep reminding viewers that "we are holding, waiting for a break in the clouds." When that break happens, the countdown can go on and the flight is launched.

Trudging down the road with my bedraggled mind not able to see past the sad memories of the day, the bell, coupled with the cookie thought and the awareness of it, provided my personal break in the clouds. Had I been able to put it into words, I might have said, "I had a free moment in which I knew that I could go back to my stories, and wander around in them again, or not. In that moment, I was able to say, 'I am out of here.' "

And here is an important caveat, especially if you are thinking of an issue in your life, right now, that seems to be surrounded by impenetrable clouds. "Free moments" in an upset mind seem to me to be instances of grace, the attention detached from its troubles—at least for a moment—by a compelling diversion, enough awareness to notice the escape route, and enough energy to take it. For issues that the mind is particularly reluctant to face, or for emotional responses so complex or long-standing that no amount of "I'm out of here" works, gentle, patient attention will be more appropriate than dint-of-will effort. That comes next. It's Wise Mindfulness.

WISE
MINDFULNESS

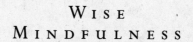

Tidying the Mind: How Mindfulness
Cultivates Wisdom

Nyanaponika Thera (*thera* means "elder monk"), a native German Jew who traveled to Sri Lanka after university and ultimately became renowned as a Buddhist scholar, teacher, and writer, describes the practice of mindfulness as "tidying the mind." The analogy that he uses to describe the state of the mind left to its own random devices is that of a messy living room. I love that. It tickles me to think of an old renunciative monk in Sri Lanka describing his insights after decades of practice in language that sounds like a European housewife of a hundred years ago. I imagine a Victorian parlor with brocade upholstery and ornately carved chair backs, fringed lampshades, bookshelves lining the walls, and bric-a-brac and travel memorabilia on all the end tables. With everything accounted for, properly organized, it would be crowded, but also interesting and even inviting. If it were messy, you might not find a comfortable place to sit down. It would be hard to relax. If you were looking for something, it might be hidden behind something else.

The living room of my own mind, unless I keep tidying it, is not a relaxing place. It easily becomes cluttered with old, tedious stories, with the few embarrassing secrets I don't like being reminded of, and with an assortment of screens—like foldable shoji screens—that block out, or specifically let in, what my peripheral mind vision chooses for me to see. Even when I am consciously trying to notice what's going on around me, I know that my mind automatically selects the material it wants to report and how—much like a newspaper—it slants the data. I think everyone's mind does the same thing. Here is an example from my experience as a hint for how to read your own mind.

My husband and I were driving home late one afternoon, and as we drove around a familiar bend on the rural road that leads to our home, I noticed that both the car and the pickup truck that were usually parked outside the house on that corner were not there. The dog that lives in that house was lying in the driveway, head down over one of his paws. I saw what looked to me like dark swerve marks on the gray asphalt road.

"Stop!" I said to Seymour. "The dog has been hit by a car, and his owners aren't home. His paw has been hurt. Look! Isn't that blood over there? Those smudges near the swerve marks? Let's go back. We'll need to call the Humane Society."

"The dog is fine. He's just lying there. He's always there."

"Yes, but usually he picks up his head."

"He's resting. What's the matter with you?"

"Let's go back. What if he really is wounded? What if he bleeds to death? I'll have it on my conscience. Turn the car around." We drove back. As we pulled into the driveway, the dog stood up and wagged his tail.

"Okay," I said, "he's fine. Now let's get out of the driveway before the owners come back and find us here. But really, don't you see swerve marks there?"

There were swerve marks. There are many swerve marks on that road. It has lots of sharp turns. It was the combination of the swerve marks and the lying-down dog and the missing cars that were the three pieces of data that my mind—a mind cluttered by a story called (perhaps) "Someone will die and I will have been the cause of it"—used to create a reality.

I don't know how that particular story got installed in my mind. An analogous real-life experience never happened to me. I could hypothesize—"I must have thought . . . ," "Perhaps I imagined . . . ," "In a previous lifetime . . ."—but really, I don't know. I do know that my mind selects the data it expects to see.

And that story is not the only piece of permanent hardware in my mind. "People will like me" is another view that shapes my experience, and although I think it's there because my parents and grandparents loved me a lot, that conclusion itself is part of the workings of my mind, informed as it is by developmental psychology. "I love Mozart," "I don't like celery," "I'm a morning person," "I startle easily," and "I can't carry a tune" are also all part of the database of my mind—along with probably a zillion other pieces of information—through which incoming data needs to make its way to whatever place intentions for response are born. I think the sorting and screening apparatus of my mind is pretty much in there for good for this lifetime. If I pay attention to it all, I won't trip over it. I'll be able to make good—or good enough—decisions.

Also, whatever hardware it is that causes me to stop for lying-down dogs, I'm content to have it. Who knows? I may even be making a mistake in identifying the hardware. Maybe it's not "Someone will die and it will be my fault" (a guilt-inspired formulation) as much as "I am a caring person and even the suggestion of distress awakens my attention." I like that story better. Anyway, everyone has stories, and that particular one doesn't disrupt my life. Even if I periodically check on a perfectly healthy dog (or cat or person or any other being that looks as if it might need help), the kindness that motivated my stopping to check, especially if it is followed by the discovery that all is well, is a pick-me-up for my mind, a mental refresher. It feels good.

Indeed, the thesis of this whole book, from the beginning, has been that restoring caring connection when it is disrupted, and maintaining it when it is present, is happiness. Not even, leads to happiness. Equals happiness. With that as my core belief, mindfulness of the presence of (or the absence of and the subsequent intention to restore) caring connection is, for me, the key element of practice. Mindfulness of everything, of the physical body, or of the breath specifically, or of thoughts or feelings or emotional responses—the objects of attention that the Buddha lists in his classic instruction sermon The Foundations of Mindfulness—condition the mind to notice the presence or absence of caring connection and the difference that that connection makes. Here's an example:

In 1986, in the early afternoon of the midpoint day of a two-week mindfulness retreat on the south coast of the big island of Hawaii, the bell to end the meditation period rang only ten minutes after the session had begun. The retreat manager announced that she'd been notified by the Civil Defense office in Hilo that an earthquake off the coast of Japan had caused a tidal wave. The wave was crossing the ocean in our direction and was projected to arrive in three hours. "We have seventy people here," she said, "and only one car. Since there are no available buses to send from Hilo," she continued, "and we can't leave, the Civil Defense told us to take high ground and organize our supplies in case we get stranded."

We were living in two-story bungalows on a beach ringed by thick jungle. The best we could do to "take high ground" was go upstairs. We collected matches, boxes of crackers and crates of fruit, mosquito repellent, and flashlights and brought them to the room we were using as our communal meditation space, the second floor of the largest bungalow. We filled the bathtubs with fresh water lest the water pipes burst. When we had finished preparing, we took our seats around the room. Most of us, facing our teacher, were also facing a wall-to-wall window that looked out across the sea to the flat horizon.

The teacher, Joseph Goldstein, told the story of a Zen master of long ago who was asked, "What would you do if the waters of the north and the south and the east and the west all rose around you?" The Zen master, Joseph continued, was reported to have said, "I would just sit."

Then Joseph said, "Let's sit."

I closed my eyes and then opened them again, checking the horizon. I felt my heart pounding. I wonder how I'd feel if I were in that situation today, with the images of the recent devastating tsunami in the Indian Ocean in my mind. I remember that at the time, imagining what a wall of water moving toward us would look like, I was terrified. I closed my eyes and noticed that the room felt unusually quiet. I took a breath and felt it enough to have it catch my attention.

I suppose out of habit, I began to name my experience to myself: Breath in, breath out. Breath in, breath out. It's very quiet. My hands are cold. My heart is pounding. I am trembling. I heard my mind saying, "I don't want to drown," and also, "Take a breath, Sylvia. Now another one." I noticed my mind quieting down as I named breaths. "In. Out. In. Out." I remember feeling surprised to find that my hands felt warmer and my heart had stopped pounding. "Maybe the tidal wave will happen," I thought. "Maybe not. I don't know."

Realizing that I didn't know provided a moment of relief.

I opened my eyes. It was windy outside, and I could see

the palms swaying. I noticed that one man was watching the sea with binoculars, and I recall feeling touched by that, imagining him thinking that his checking close-up could make a difference. My good friend James was sitting next to me. I thought about James's pregnant wife, Jane, at home in Berkeley, and I suddenly wanted very much for us all to survive so that James could be home when his child was born. James's hands were folded in his lap, as were mine. I reached over and tapped his knee and held out my hand. He reached for it, and we both closed our eyes and sat for a long while, holding hands. I noticed my friend Len, an executive with KCBS in San Francisco, sitting across the room, and I thought, "If we survive, Len should be the first to use the phone. He could let the radio station know that we're all okay, and then KCBS could broadcast that news across the country to reassure all the relatives who would be worrying about us."

The tidal wave never arrived. It passed south of Hawaii. It's more than twenty years now since that day, and I find that when I remember the event, or tell it as a story, the drama of it—"Can you *imagine* . . . ?"—is not what I think about. After all, we did survive. What continues to inspire me, as I recall or recount that day, is how my experience changed when I was able to shift my attention from personal fear to our communal lot. We were all threatened. We all wanted to live. We all had family or friends who loved us. The outcome of our situation was completely out of our control. And I cared. Of course I cared about myself, and I thought about my family and hoped they would not lose me. But I realized that I felt better—as if a burden had shifted— when I thought about other people's families, too. Perhaps that's the clue about the happiness inherent in caring connections. The frightened "I" who struggles is replaced by the "we" who do this difficult life together, looking after one another. Holding hands.

Correcting the View:
Wise Mindfulness as a Reality Check

I am particularly fond of a definition of mindfulness that I discovered in a French translation of an English-language book on Buddhism. The English term had been *seeing clearly,* and the translation was *vision profonde.* When I explain that to mindfulness students, I say, "If I wipe my eyeglasses, I might see clearly, but my vision might be superficial." I explain that mindfulness, to me, means seeing profoundly, seeing what is beyond my immediate impression of what's happening to a level of discriminating awareness that leads to skillful response. My immediate impressions are often limited.

Here's a story that I heard from my friend Jeff, who is a traditionally observant Jew as well as a mediator for corporate disputes and whose clients are often businesses that are related to religious observance. He told the story in a meditation class I was teaching to corroborate a point I had just made. I'd mentioned the mindfulness bell that is rung in certain Buddhist communities at unscheduled times in the day. At the sound of the bell, all activities stop. The community sits or stands or anyway stays still for two or three minutes, until the bell rings again. Then everyone resumes whatever they were doing. It is a time meant for, literally, "catching one's breath," paying attention to the breath as a break from activity to be sure that one's mind is clear and one's perspective is unconfused.

Jeff told the group that he had recently had a similar experience while attempting to negotiate an agreement between two rival businesses, each of which felt that it had been genuinely wronged by the other.

"The meeting went on for days," he said, "and each side brought their lawyers and an enormous amount of evidence to back up their claims. The discussions were often intense. Tempers got shorter and shorter. Then, at some point every afternoon, someone would announce, 'It's time to *daven*

Mincha' (to pray the afternoon liturgy), and everyone would stop, face toward the east, and chant together. That prayer session," Jeff concluded, "takes less than ten minutes altogether, and when we returned to negotiating, every-thing went much better."

As Jeff told his story, I thought, "Everyone had a reality check. They remembered that they were adversaries, not enemies." I loved visualizing everyone standing up and mov-ing from facing one another across a table to facing in the same direction. "Literally," I thought, "they could see that they are all on 'the same side,' people with shared ideals who have—at the moment—differing opinions."

Jeff's description of an afternoon "prayer break," like a mindfulness bell break, a yoga asana break, or a walk-around-the-block break, are all examples of comforting and soothing opportunities—because they are familiar and re-quire no effort other than attention—to give tense, con-fused, tired, anxious minds a chance to relax and regroup. One image that comes to my mind is that of football players taking a time-out when they have possession of the ball within scoring distance, are behind by two points, and have ten seconds left in the game. I don't know what the quarter-back is saying in that huddle—perhaps suggesting a field goal attempt—but I like to imagine he is saying, "Breathe. Calm down. Remember that you know how to do this." I'm even hopeful some quarterbacks say, "It's just a game. Don't hurt anyone."

Living mindfully does not mean living slowly, and stopping for a reality check can be an instantaneous, invisible event. The key question that I ask myself when I realize that my mind is caught in turmoil—unable to establish a caring connection with myself or anyone or anything else—is, "What's really happening? What is the bigger picture?" I am fascinated by the new TV technical options that, with a click of the remote control, allow a person to watch the Army-Navy game in a little box at the lower left of the screen at the same time that the Notre Dame–USC game continues all around it on the rest of the screen. I see that my own mind functions much the same way. The story of the unfolding world is happening on my big screen, and *My Life* is showing in my little box. When my little-box drama becomes intense—with pain or even with unexpected joy—it swells up and fills the whole screen. I forget the world altogether. It happens to me all the time. It's normal and natural.

It's only if my view stays locked on the small screen that I suffer. If I can't see around my personal story, I'll have no way to see it in context: This is one event in a life of events. It is whatever it is, but it is temporal. This pain is terrible, but it won't last. I can manage it. Or this joy is incredible, but it won't last. Celebrate it now!

I also won't be able to see my story in the context of one of six billion or so human stories all showing simultaneously as part of the great epic called Life on Earth. I am sure that if I had a God's-eye view in place of a my-eye view, I would be nothing but amazed: Multitudes coming and going, being born and dying, eating and sleeping and playing and singing and arguing and fighting and killing and making truces, over and over again. And the earth itself greening and dying and greening and dying endlessly, exactly on schedule.

Whenever, for me, the sense of I disappears into the awareness of us, there is no one left to suffer. There is no "I" who needs anything. The words that come to mind are "My cup is brimming." And nothing needs to be rejected: "This is the way it is. I am an actor in this giant cosmic movie, not the director." It is a blessed shift of perspective, a great personal relief, and it is as near as this next moment's breath.

Try this now. Keep your eyes open, even keep reading these instructions, but let your attention rest on the sensations of the breath coming in and out of your body, especially around your rib cage. You'll feel the sense of stretching and expansion in your muscles, maybe even the way your arms are lifted up a bit as inhalation happens.

You'll notice the sense of rib cage and muscles and arms all settling down again as exhalation happens. In just a moment, when you finish reading this last instruction, I hope you'll close your eyes and, continuing to rest the attention in the sensations of breath, notice how breathing happens all by itself. No "one" breathes alone. Breathing is happening in this body and every other living thing, everything literally sharing one giant breath. An animal body breathing produces carbon dioxide, which some nearby tree or fern or grass breathes in and exhales as oxygen so another animal can breathe it in. Nothing lives alone.

It's Easy to Become Confused: How Mindfulness Creates Clarity

It's incredibly easy to become confused. The mind becomes overwhelmed—by a challenge or its impulsive response to a challenge—and becomes confused, misreads what's happening, and frightens itself.

Mindfulness doesn't erase confusion as much as it notices it and dissolves, or at least reduces, the fear about it. As fear lessens, misperceptions begin to correct themselves. And opportunities for correction—which, allowing myself a slight pun, are also opportunities for connection—are always available.

Here's a story:

I was traveling on the Metroliner express train between Washington, D.C., and New York City one morning, and although it was early and I had bought several newspapers I wanted to read, not long into the trip I felt an enormous wave of exhaustion come over me. Probably I was just tired—I had been traveling and teaching, a new city every other day—but my mind, as it often does, made a story out of it. "You are too old to be doing this. Look at all these energetic young people in this train, clicking away on computers. They feel excited about working today. They are not worrying about being too tired. They are not worried about the world. They aren't thinking—as I am—'What's the use of doing anything with the news as terrible as it is?' "

I turned to the woman sitting next to me. I had checked her out as we began the trip. Thirty-something. Chic red suit. Very good haircut. Well-done makeup. Elegant attaché case tucked under the seat in front of her. Reading *Vogue* magazine.

"Excuse me," I said. "I am very tired, and I need to sleep. I'd like to get up, though, twenty minutes before Penn Station. Will you wake me, please?"

"Yes, of course," she answered, and then, leaning toward

me, brow furrowed in concern, she asked, "Are you all right?"

"Yes," I said. "I'm all right. Are you?"

"No," she said. "I'm not."

I felt a *zap* of rousing energy run through me that I remember as literally sitting me up in my seat and certainly clearing my mind of fogginess.

"You want to talk?"

"I do," she answered. "I read the same newspaper you were reading just now, at home, before I left. In Washington, you live in the middle of politics, and you stop believing anyone. I have two young children. I don't know how they can grow up in this world."

We talked about politics and ideologies and how her family had influenced her political views and how mine had influenced me. Then we talked about where we'd grown up, where our parents and grandparents had come from. Everyone has a story.

"I'm also worried," she went on, "about the meeting I'm going to in New York today." She explained that although she worked in Washington, where she lived, the main office of the company she worked for was in New York and she felt that keeping her job depended on the presentation she would make that day. As she explained the work she did, and I listened, I was hearing a parallel voice in my own mind saying, "Look how you put the data together all wrong, Sylvia. You added up the suit and the attaché case and her age and you decided that she was naïve and indifferent to the heavy concerns of the world. You decided that about all the other energetic-looking people on this train. Only you, you thought, are thinking of the pain of the world. This is ageism in reverse! How could you fall into that?"

I could listen to my mind, and the young woman talking, at the same time because I was awake and enjoying myself. I was awake because my mind, previously blurred by the fog of fatigue and the depressing story I had been telling myself, had been rescued from its downward spiral by someone else saying, "No, I'm not all right." The startle in my mind, brought on by her statement of distress, was a mindfulness bell. My self-preoccupied story could stop, and connection with her could happen. Of course I wished wholeheartedly that everything would work out for her in her life, but I think the chief cause of my happiness was realizing, "My heart is alive! I care! And I am never—even in my most discouraged moments—really alone."

Walking out of Penn Station, I realized we'd never told each other our names. It didn't matter. I thought about how everyone carries their family and their work and the whole world around with them all the time and that saying "Are you all right?" is like throwing someone a rescue rope that says, "Want to connect?" I also realized I was singing to myself "I know that my redeemer liveth . . ." from *The Messiah*—it was Christmas season, and maybe it was on some public-address system—and I thought, "My redeemer is *always* the person next to me."

And It's Particularly Easy to Get Angry: How Mindfulness Dispels Aversion

The important thing about noticing the mind's editorial opinions, "I like it" or "I don't like it," is that unwelcome experiences, the "I don't like it" experiences, often arouse what traditional texts call aversion, the impulse in the mind to distance itself from an unpleasant situation. The unpleasant situation is painful, the impulse to distance is painful, and being disconnected—not in a cordial relationship with whatever is happening—is also painful. And still, it's easy to get angry. I'm a mild-mannered person, but inside, even if I don't show it, I get annoyed if I want something and I'm not getting it. I get annoyed at myself if I don't do something as well as I had hoped to. I get irritated at my mind for its periodic fugues of worry even though I recognize them as habits for which I am not to blame. I recently even watched as my mind got mad at a squirrel who was eating out of my bird feeder—I would have happily fed it squirrel food, had I anticipated its arrival—but I was expecting birds. You expect one thing, and . . .

I was one of the six thousand people in the campus theater of the University of California–Irvine listening to a talk by the Dalai Lama on the day after it had been announced that he was the recipient of that year's Nobel Peace Prize, when someone asked him, "Do you ever get angry?"

"Of course," he responded, seeming to find the question funny and laughing his now familiar "Heh-heh-heh-heh" chuckle. "Something happens. It isn't what you expected. Anger arises. But, you know, it doesn't have to be a problem. Heh-heh-heh-heh."

I think it's the "not what you expected," startle factor that throws the mind off balance—broadsides it, is what I think—so that it gets confused, then bewildered, then frightened, and then angry. If something can happen to dispel the confusion, there won't be a problem.

Here's a story about startle and anger—again, from my own experience, but I'm hoping that you'll think, as you read it, "What is my story that matches this one?" I remembered, in the middle of this event unfolding, hearing the Dalai Lama's voice saying, "Something happens. It isn't what you expected. Anger arises."

I had been very glad, and proud, to have been asked to help plan the design for the contemplative floor—meditation room and adjacent silent library space—that was being included in the building of a new Jewish Community Center in Manhattan, in New York City. Space set apart for meditation was, in 2000, a unique addition to traditionally designed community centers, and everyone involved with the project was excited about it. The inaugural use of the meditation room was a daylong retreat for rabbis that I co-led with my friend Sheila Weinberg.

The morning session passed easily from times of instruction to periods of silent sitting meditation to times of walking, as a group, in a slow circle around the perimeter of the room. Sheila and I gave instructions, and people asked questions and we answered them. I was pleased to note that the tenor of the discourse became more leisurely as people seemed to settle into paying attention, moment to moment, to their experience. By lunchtime, the atmosphere in the room seemed to me palpably more relaxed. We gave instructions for Eating Meditation—in essence, "Pay attention to the sensations of eating along with all the thoughts and feelings that arise about the experience"—and repaired to the library next door where a buffet lunch had been set out. People went through the line silently and sat at the library tables to eat. Most people chose seats that looked out the windows so they could watch the rain. I did, too.

Then I heard a conversation happening on the other side of the wall that divided the library and meditation room space from the rest of the seventh floor:

"Three hearts beats three diamonds."

I wasn't sure I'd heard correctly.

"That's right. Three hearts beats three diamonds. Everyone knows that."

"What *is* that?" I heard my mind preparing a protest. "This is meant to be a contemplative space. This is the meditation floor." I noticed that the wall designer had left spaces between the rooms at the edges of each wall. "What were they thinking? No one should be hearing anything, let alone card game conversation." I walked to the end of the dividing wall and peeked through the space. Old men and women playing cards. I sat back down and noticed that the other people in the room all seemed to be watching the rain and eating their lunch. I was about to eat mine when I heard the sound of shuffling feet behind me. I turned and saw several elderly people—undoubtedly the card players—helping themselves to the food on our buffet.

My mind thought, "The last straw! That is our food." I looked around to see if the program director of the center, a participant in the retreat, was there. I thought I'd let her handle the situation.

In the several seconds it took to pick her out—who knows, maybe it was the steady sound of the rain drilling on the windows or the sight of so many friends and colleagues contentedly eating—I changed my mind. Or it changed itself. The indignation that had filled it—"Our silence." "Our food"—disappeared. Right now, remembering the moment, I think it was the pleasure I felt at seeing so many people I loved feeling good that soothed my ruffled mind and let its own wisdom take over.

There were two wisdoms, the situational wisdom and the eternal wisdom. The situational wisdom went like this: These are elderly people, living in nearby apartments, who would otherwise be indoors in this weather and are probably eager for company. Here they can meet and play and spend the day happily. Of course I want them to be here. And there is plenty of food. We've all had our portions. If someone told me that there were homeless people outside this building on Amsterdam Avenue who needed this food, I would surely carry it downstairs. Why not share it with these bridge players?

Why not, indeed? I think my mind, somewhat proprietary about "the space I planned and the program I designed," jumped to the conclusion that the "disruption" of noises next door would upset the relaxed mind states we'd all been cultivating and that the good feeling I hoped people would report at the end of the day wouldn't happen. "My" day wasn't going the way I had planned. I suppose my ego, hoping for a personal reward, had a moment of frenzy thinking it wouldn't happen. I'm not even sure that it was the realization that my ego was involved that calmed my mind back into clarity. Maybe it was my view of my friends looking happy that assured my ego of its reward. Maybe both.

And here is the eternal wisdom: There are always challenges. You plan for one thing, and something else often happens. The long view—is this a desirable thing or an undesirable thing?—is rarely immediately apparent. Immediate emotional responses are just that. Noticing them, and reflecting, is always a good idea. And the cause of suffering—always—is struggling with challenge rather than responding with sound judgment and kindness.

Once More, with Feeling:
Liberating the Mind from Secrets

Now I want to go back to a remark I made earlier—"It's hard to be hiding from thoughts on retreat, and it's hard to be hiding from them in life"—so I can describe mindfulness as the process of liberating the mind from secrets that it's trying to keep hidden because it's afraid, or embarrassed, to face them. Unlike the spontaneous confusing reactions to challenge that we all experience—those that arise and pass in response to startling situations—I think we each have an idiosyncratic assortment of view-distorting stories etched into our neurology of which we are unaware and which are therefore an ongoing source of confusion. When my mind, at ease, has allowed fragments of past experience that my psyche had hidden from me into my conscious mind for a more contemporary encounter, I have been all the better for it.

And I want to add this caveat: not every past trauma needs to be revived and relived. (Whew! Given the number of dreadful moments in any life, we'd never get caught up!) What my mind has swallowed up, and is keeping quiet about, I'm happy to not notice. I am, however, very willing to discover habits of my mind that require energy in order to stay hidden. I don't think in terms of healing my mind—

I prefer thinking that its habits are its habits, not illnesses—but I do want to know what's there so I don't misjudge current experience because I am seeing it through a lens I didn't notice.

Do you remember the story of my concern about the lying-down dog? My guess is that my habit of stopping to check "Is everything okay?" has multiple causes. I imagine that it is at least partly my natural good-heartedness. It's also, I think, a derivative of a generalized tendency to worry that I seem to have had since birth. It's probably also habitual anxiety from years of alarm I had about my mother's fragile health during my childhood. Or maybe it's something else I haven't yet discovered. Or all of them together. The etiology of my habit doesn't seem nearly as important to me as the fact that I can see it. It is not hidden. I can work with it or work around it. It isn't—normally—problematic. The secrets of my psyche that I hide from myself—that any of us hide from ourselves—become problematic when they inform, in an undercover way, how we think about ourselves and other people and how we behave.

I think when Nyanaponika Thera uses the phrase "tidying the mind," it includes sweeping secrets out from behind screens in the mind and examining them in the daylight of current, relaxed reflection.

Here's a story:

My friend Elaine (who said I could tell this story if I changed her name) is in her late fifties, a longtime meditator who takes a few weeks each year out of her professional and family life to be on retreat. She told me, on the last evening of a ten-day retreat, that on that very morning, as she had approached the glass doors of the main meditation hall at Spirit Rock Center, she'd seen her reflection in the glass and heard her mind say, "I do *not* have bowed legs!"

When Elaine reported that moment to me, she said that she'd been surprised. She remembered her mother, forty or so years ago, telling her that her legs were bowed, but she also told me that she hadn't thought about it in a very long time.

"Then," she continued, "after I sat down to meditate, my mind rolled out what seemed like a long audiotape of other critical remarks that my mother had made about my appearance as a child and then as a teenager. All grouped together, I felt it like one blow after another. I wonder," Elaine added, "if this is the very pain I'd felt at the time of those insults that somehow got stored in my brain along with the memories. The worst, though," she concluded, "is realizing how hard my mind has been working to hide all this from me, for so long . . . That's really sad!"

Elaine told me that she cried, on and off, for much of

the day, each time the memories replayed, sometimes as new memories were added. She said she'd also thought a lot, with her mind at ease in between bouts of crying, about how her mother's opinions, secretly hidden in her memory, had never allowed her—mirrors, compliments, and conventional standards notwithstanding—to recognize herself as being attractive. "I'm a good-looking woman," she said, laughing suddenly at her bold disclosure, "and my mother missed seeing it. Probably she didn't see herself right either," Elaine added, "so I can't even be mad at her."

This would be an amazing story if it ended with the news that negative self-images never again arose in Elaine's mind after that revelatory experience. The mind doesn't work that way, though. Opinions embedded in neurons take a long time to erase. Maybe they never entirely erase. Still, it's a great story. Elaine tells me that what happens now, since her attention has become attuned to hearing the disparaging opinions her own mind makes about how she looks—the echoes of her mother's voice so many years ago—is that she can put them aside. "I feel a bit dismayed," she says, "each time I hear them. I think about how hard my mind had to work to avoid facing what it remembered as being painful. I'm impressed, though," she continued, "with how patiently my mind waited for a time when it thought I could deal with it, for a quiet enough moment for me to re-member and look and notice that my legs aren't bowed at all."

Elaine's story is unique to her, of course, but the general experience of discovering, without explicitly calling it to mind, pieces of hidden personal history, is not unique. The particulars of everyone's stories are different, but the ele-ment of "This was something I could not have faced before, but now I can" is a common theme. The experience of "fac-ing it" is different for everyone as well. Some people, like Elaine, report a major shift in how they feel in a short time. Another friend of mine, a colleague telling me about en-countering the considerable sadness of her childhood dur-ing a period of intensive meditation in her midthirties, said, "I cried for nine months. Then, I felt better." It seems that peace of mind arrives in its own time.

And everyone manages what needs to be kept hidden as best he or she can. I have a huge respect for the mind's abil-ity to "forget" what it thinks it cannot bear to face, and really, I'm not sure that it leaves lives emotionally circum-scribed. My mother's parents decided never to mention their six-year-old daughter who died of rheumatic heart disease. I did not find out about that child until I was sixty years old, and then, only by tracking down an odd hint I'd had from my mother years before. When I asked my aunt Miriam, by then my only remaining living older relative, why no one—not even my grandfather, the child's father, whom I asked when he was very old—had told me, she said, "They forgot."

When I protested, "You don't forget a child that died!" she answered, "You do if you think you can't stand it."

I used to say—although I wouldn't now—that mindfulness practice gives a person the chance to discover that we can, in fact, stand what seems unbearable. I don't know if that's true for everyone. Everyone is different. What I do know, though, is that when, each year, a practitioner at Spirit Rock, a woman whose teenage daughter took her own life some ten years ago, a woman who has spent a lot of retreat time facing her pain, commemorates the anniversary of her child's death by ringing the big gong outside our meditation hall one hundred and eight times, I imagine she is ringing it for my grandmother, too.

I began my own meditation practice fifteen years after my first experience of being in psychotherapy and ten years after I'd begun to practice as a therapist. I was therefore somewhat surprised to find that, especially on retreat, as soon as I was able to relax and focus my mind, all of my "issues," themes that I thought I had reconciled as part of my own therapy, returned like slain villains in operettas to take yet another curtain call bow. I thought, "What is *this*? I know about this. I did this already!"

For some years, my villains returned with more reenactments of their roles and more curtain calls. I think what was true was that although I knew what issues had been most difficult for me in my life, I may not have known the depth of the feelings I had about them. Maybe I knew *about* them more than I felt how much they had terrified me or grieved me. When those stories, with their feelings, returned—especially if I was on retreat and had enough time, and enough composure, to "sit" with them—I paid attention to them. What I tell people now is, "Try to keep your mind hospitable. This needs to visit for a while. Don't be afraid."

My conclusion about my own experience is that some combination of having been ten years older, having the support of a silent community around me, and having been able to keep my mind alert and balanced through experiences of "once more, with feeling," changed my not quite slain villains into ghosts that don't haunt. Most of the time. When they do—if, for whatever reason, my mind is overwhelmed and vulnerable to stress—I recognize them and work around them.

Keeping the Mind Noncontentious:
Metta Practice as Wise Mindfulness

When I was introduced to *metta* practice twenty-five years ago, I was told that it was different—not only in technique but also in goal—from mindfulness. In fact, it was—and still sometimes is—presented as an ancillary practice to use in case of special needs such as perilous circumstances or as a formal ritual ending for retreat practice, part of a dedication of merit. What I have come to believe, out of my experience, is that mindfulness and *metta*—although they are associated with different techniques—are, each of them, integral to the practice of the other. I cannot be genuinely mindful—open to my moment-to-moment experience without hesitation or hiding—unless my mind is benevolent, unless I forgive whatever part of my experience arouses distress in me. Indeed, it is the mindful awareness "I'm in pain," or someone else is, that causes feelings of goodwill to spontaneously arise in me. And I couldn't be seriously practicing *metta* without paying very careful attention to—being mindful of—whether what I am wishing matches what I feel. In my experience, it's the repeated direct awareness of how benevolent connection—friendliness, compassion, appreciation—liberates my mind from suffering that supports both wisdom and equanimity in me and inspires my determination to stay alert.

In fact, a favorite prayer of mine is, "May I meet this moment fully. May I meet it as a friend." I think of it as an everyday, ongoing, whole-life practice, a combination of mindfulness and *metta* that recognizes that both are necessary to keep my mind relaxed and friendly even when it is startled. Sometimes I say it to myself just once, as a reminder, in a situation where suddenly I am feeling challenged and need a momentary balancing break before continuing. Sometimes I use it as a mantra, in sitting meditation, and then I say it silently to myself, again and again. Perhaps you'd like to stop reading now, just for a few minutes, and try it. If you will be repeating it as a meditative mantra, perhaps you could say the first phrase as you breathe in and the second as you breathe out. "May I meet this moment fully. May I meet it as a friend."

The Truth about Preferences: The *Metta* Riddle

Mindfulness is often defined as the attention meeting the moment with balanced awareness. For the awareness to stay balanced, it needs to be able to notice what's happening, to register whether it is pleased or not, and to behave as if it had no preferences—to stay noncontentious—even though, the truth is, we *always* have preferences. It's the same with *metta*. We go around in our lives meeting people—in thought or in person—who register in the mind with a charge of "pleasant" or "unpleasant," and the mind instinctively is either attracted or annoyed. Again, for the mind to stay peaceful, a repository of wisdom, it needs to behave as if it had no preferences, even though, again, it always does.

There are people who are dearer to me than others. Probably it's part of our neurology, a key to survival. When the last big earthquake hit San Francisco on a fall evening in 1989, the very first thing I did when I felt the shock roll under my house was look at my watch. I wanted to know what time it was so I could reassure myself that my family members, all coming home from work or school at that hour, were not on a bridge. When I figured out that they were likely past the bridges—that "my people" were not in jeopardy—I turned on the TV to check how everyone else was managing.

I don't think any of that is a mistake. I think we are wired for intimacy. Indeed, I think it is my preferences, and my awareness of them, that ultimately connect me to other people. I know that however much I say *metta* prayers for all beings—which I do, as part of formal *metta* practice—I notice how ardency and fervor become part of my prayers if they are for people with whom I am personally involved. I understand—at least theoretically—that if I were totally poised about the outcome of all situations, I wouldn't have preferences and I'd never have the pain of disappointment. But still . . .

My phone rang just after six o'clock on a winter morning of very heavy rain and high winds. It was my husband, Seymour, calling. He'd left an hour earlier to do his freeway commute before the traffic got heavy, and I'd gone back to bed and fallen asleep.

"Have you heard the news yet?"

"What news? I've been sleeping. What happened?"

"Well," he said, "they aren't saying names yet, but one of the rescue helicopters from Santa Rosa crashed this morning on its way to Fort Bragg. The pilot and the two nurses on board were killed."

In Sonoma County, California, there are three pilots and six nurses who rotate days flying to administer medical care to people at accident sites or people with medical crises who live in remote places and need to be rushed to the hospital. Our friend Laura was one of the six nurses. She'd told us amazing stories about rescues of hikers stranded halfway down cliffs over the Pacific beaches or last-minute airlifts of women in labor to hospitals equipped to handle premature births.

"Oh, please, God," I said, "may it not be Laura."

"I know," Seymour replied. "I thought the same thing."

"When will they announce who it was? Did they say?"

"No, all they said was that the weather was so bad there was no visibility, and the helicopter crashed into a mountainside near Fort Bragg and everyone on board was killed."

"I can't call George this early," I said. "I'll wait until eight. I'll call you and let you know."

I sat in the chair in the corner of my living room next to the window that looks out to the east. I sit there most mornings to watch the sunrise. The sky was still dark, and it was still raining. I heard the competing messages in my mind: "Please, let it not be Laura." And, "What has happened has already happened. Pray for the people who died. Pray for the people they leave behind." And, again, "Please, please, let it not be Laura."

I imagined Levi and Sofie, Laura's eight-year-old twins, without their mother, and it was a terrible thought. I imagined George without Laura. I heard my alternating petitions, "May all beings be comforted" and "Please, not Laura." I thought about the pilots and nurses whom I did not know and realized that each of them, in his or her way, was somebody's Laura. I waited until eight o'clock to phone, and Laura answered.

There is a riddle in classical Buddhist literature. It is presented as the question that teachers ask students to test the level of the students' wisdom and compassion. It goes like this:

You are walking in a forest with your teacher, your best-beloved friend, a familiar stranger about whom you have neutral feelings, and your worst enemy. Suddenly, an armed desperado leaps out into your path and threatens to kill everyone unless you choose one of the five travelers—you are included with the other four—to be sacrificed. Then the rest of the party can proceed.

I've posed this riddle to lots of classes, and I've found that people make choices in all but one category:

"I would choose myself. If I made any other choice, I couldn't live with myself."

"I would choose my teacher. She had great equanimity and would be the one most able to handle dying."

"I would choose the neutral person. It would be a choice without passion, so maybe it would be a lesser karmic offense."

"I would choose my enemy. I wouldn't like to do it, but let's get real. That's the obvious choice."

Sometimes people say, "I couldn't choose. I wouldn't be able to differentiate." That, I understand, is the "right" answer to the riddle, the one that shows that your heart has been cleansed of all partiality. In my experience, when someone offers the "I couldn't choose" response, the rest of the class calls out, "No fair! The riddle says you have to choose." And someone will often call out, "Of *course* you can choose."

No one, in my experience, has ever said, "I would choose my best-beloved friend." For every other category, there is an explanation. For what is dearest to one's heart, there simply isn't.

In fact, in the *Metta Sutta,* the Buddha's Sermon on Lovingkindness, there is this line:

> *Just as a mother protects with her life*
> *Her child, her only child,*
> *So with a boundless heart*
> *Should one cherish all living beings*
> *Radiating kindness over the entire world.*

I think this points explicitly to the fact that our closest bonds are the source of our concern for all living beings, even those we don't know, even the people we may designate as enemies. Isn't it true for you—as it is for me—that when you hear about someone who has been bereaved, your heart is moved by what you intuit he or she must be feeling? We all know what "bereft" feels like. What moves my mind to concern and compassion for people I don't know—or perhaps don't even like—is knowing that everyone loves their Laura as much as I do mine.

One Breath, One Name: Mindful Blessing

This meditation combines the traditional "breath anchor" of mindfulness practice with the ever-expanding list of benevolent wish recipients that is the basis of *metta* practice. The Foundations of Mindfulness sermon begins with attention to the breath and builds, from there, to attention to everything. The commonly used practice form for *metta* practice begins with prayers for those nearest and dearest and moves, as if through concentric orbits of connection from proximal to distal, to include prayers for everyone.

I love doing this. And I find it immediately soothing (from the calm attention to the breath) and immediately delightful (because I'm thinking of people I love and wishing them well). It's very easy.

Here's how to do it. Maybe you'll want to try it right now.

Feel yourself breathing. Don't change the breath in any way. Just notice it. In. Out. In. Out.

Now think of the prayer you'd like to say: "May you be peaceful" or "May you be happy" or "May this be a wonderful day for you" or "May you thrive in every way." Those are only some ideas. Think of anything you like, but try to think of something that you could wish for everyone in the world from your best beloved to the person who delivers your mail.

Let it be your intention—with each breath you take—that the wish you've made will be dedicated to whomever your mind remembers at that moment. Then begin your dedication of wishes. (I don't say the wish each time. With each breath, I think of someone, say the person's name to myself, and feel myself offering her or him that prayer. Then I go on to the next breath and the next person.)

My list of names changes each time I do this meditation, but Seymour—my life partner since I was fifteen years old—is the person I always think of, whose name I say to myself with my first breath. He may not be the person most on my mind at the time, or I may even be in a cross mood with him, but I've been starting this "liturgy" with him for so long it is the automatic starting word. If I take a breath

and say "Seymour" to myself, my mind will continue automatically, "Michael" (my eldest son) . . . and on through my
family and all my friends who are as dear to me as family and
so get included, as a matter of course, in my prayers. This
part of the meditation always cheers my mind. I am reminded of how many people are dear to me. Even if I am
upset by or worried about any one of them, wishing them
well, calmly and deliberately, reminds me of my concerns
and of what I can—or sometimes can't—do for them. Either way, I feel relieved. It is as if I have made the rounds of
my personal world.

After I've finished with my "regulars," I find that my
mind continues, on its own, to propose people for me to
name, one on each breath, and I do. I don't need to think
very hard. Colleagues, acquaintances, any person I know
about in some way, all "line up" in my mind in time for the
next breath. Sometimes, when my mind feels particularly
easy and playful, it can seem like a game: "Uh-oh, I am running out of people. Whom can I think of?" But there is always someone to think of. "May my brother-in-law's
business partner, who I heard is sick, also be well."

And sometimes, when I think of a person and find that
my mind balks, "Not that person!" I "stay" with that person
and with my intention to bless for however many breaths it
takes me to feel easy about it. It doesn't solve my difficulties

with that person, but it does mitigate the distress I am feeling about them. Since it's not unusual for me to find that I am harboring some hidden resentment toward someone, this "one breath, one name" meditation works like a sieve, catching and displaying the uncomfortable pieces of my life so I can be aware of them and perhaps do something about them.

Try this meditation now, okay? I think it creates as much happiness as it does because every breath draws another line of connection. But you need to try it for yourself to find that's true.

WISE
CONCENTRATION

Keeping the Mind Steady:
Wise Concentration as the Guardian of Wisdom

Wise Concentration steadies the mind as it meets and considers experiences mindfully, investigating them with *vision profonde*. And Wise Concentration is the ballast in the mind that allows for Wise Effort to operate, to catch the mind in midmistake and reroute it. All the Eightfold Path steps support one another, but I think of Wise Concentration as the fundamental support of them all. The quality I most associate with Concentration is composure.

There is a Zen story about a town being notified of the impending arrival of a notorious samurai warrior bent on destruction. The townspeople flee. The monks in the monastery flee. The abbot, according to the story, accomplished in concentration and unshakable in his equanimity—remember the story of the Buddha confronting Mara?—remains seated on his meditation cushion in the shrine room. When the warrior, having discovered the deserted town and the deserted monastery, finds the abbot at ease, his image of himself as a person worthy of inspiring terror is wounded. He brandishes his sword and shouts, "Don't you know that I am the kind of man who could run you through with my sword without batting an eye?" The abbot, responding with a slight bow and palms-pressed-together gesture of respect, replies, "And I, sir, am the kind of man who can be run through by a sword without batting an eye." The warrior, in the story, acknowledges the Zen master as his teacher and becomes his disciple.

It took me awhile, maybe years, to warm up to this story. Like other Zen stories, it is sparse in its commentary. It seemed to me, originally, to imply that living and dying were all the same to the abbot. They aren't all the same to me. Then I realized that the story doesn't say anything about how the abbot *feels* about dying. It says that if his death is inevitable, he can maintain his poise. It illustrates, again, the fundamental truth that the Buddha taught, the fact that suffering arises with the imperative in the mind to have things be different from what they are. The abbot—wisdom intact because his mind is steady—is choosing not to complicate his situation with struggle. My sense of the story is that the abbot is not so profoundly absorbed in concentration—there are concentration states that "seclude" the mind from outside awareness—as to be unaware of what's happening. I think he knows what's happening. And he chooses peace.

I think the Zen story, true or legendary notwithstanding, is meant as a reminder that even in extreme circumstances, holding the mind steady is possible. My own sense is that especially in circumstances where the outcome is clearly out of one's own hands—as it is when one's death is impending and unavoidable—the mind stays steady all by itself. It can't race around looking for alternatives when there aren't any. I think about the people on the doomed airplanes of September 11, 2001, who made phone calls saying, "I love you. Take good care of yourself." Or my friend Martha, diagnosed with pancreatic cancer just after the death of her brother, who said, "When my mind protests, 'Why me?' I feel distraught, and when I remember, 'Why *not* me? These things happen,' I feel calm." Impending death leaves no room, or time, for the mind to argue "This should be otherwise." Wisdom can prevail.

Short of as powerful a teacher as imminent death, which we hope to meet only once, the story of our lives is one of continual adjustments to change, some of them welcome and some of them not. A very old woman, the aunt of a friend of mine, having outlived both her memory and almost her entire vocabulary, remembered only two words and said them to anyone who came to visit. Her words were, *temporarily* and *unexpectedly*. I don't know if that old woman knew the meaning of those words, but the people who knew and loved her enjoy imagining that she did. After all, the fundamental truth of all experience is constant change, and the changes that require some adaptive response, the "unexpected" ones, are the ones we particularly notice because we need to figure out what to do.

Any challenge, even a small one, is a potential cause of confusion. The mind, startled by a new dilemma, "Uh-oh! What now?" most often leaps immediately forward in what—for each of us—seems to be a favorite, or at least most habitual, coping style. Do you remember earlier when I said that everyone's mind—startled by challenge— responds spontaneously with an emotional state, characteristic to him or her, that confuses it? The Buddha described these states as disturbing "energies," *kileshas* in Pali, often translated as "hindrances" in English-language texts, since they hinder the mind's capacity to clearly assess what's happening. As energies, they "ruffle the mind's surface." They distort the truth. Mindfulness, you'll recall, recognizes the presence of these confusing energies, recognizes their temporality, and sees either through them or around them so that good sense can prevail. Concentration, in my experience, dissolves hindrances. I once heard a Tibetan Buddhist teacher say, "All hindrances are self-liberating in the great space of awareness." I know that when my mind is concentrated, deeply relaxed and steady, filled with warm intention, upsetting thoughts and feelings arise, but they don't "stick."

Here is a contemporary *kilesha* story. It's a good example of what happens when upsetting thoughts and feelings do "stick." I love that as it evolved at a Wednesday class at Spirit Rock Meditation Center, many of us present knew, as we heard different people contribute to the conversation, that we were developing a perfect list of the traditional five hindrances that the Buddha described.

A woman said, "Yesterday, when I went out of my apartment building in San Francisco to go to work, I noticed that I seemed to be inserting my key into my car door at a lower level than usual. Then I noticed that all four tires had been stolen during the night and my car was sitting on its hubs. I got so upset I walked to Stonestown Shopping Mall—it's only three blocks from where I live—and I bought the pair of silk pajamas I had seen several days ago in Macy's window and had been coveting. Then I went home and called the police."

"You did that?" a man asked, sounding surprised. "I

would have gone back into the house, found the superintendent, and given her a piece of my mind. A part of my rent is supposed to go for security around that building. Then I would have gone to work and probably have given everyone else a bad time. When I am mad, I lose patience with everyone."

Someone else said, "I can't take that kind of stress. I would have gone back into my apartment, called my work, told them that I was having a bad day and needed the day off. I'd have told them I'd be in tomorrow. Then I guess I would have called the police."

A woman who had been a member of the class for a long time laughingly said, "Well, I guess you can all imagine my response. I would have thought, 'Today the tires, tomorrow the whole car.' My motto," she continued, "is, 'When you aren't sure, worry.' " Everyone laughed.

And yet another person added, "I would have given myself a bad time for picking the neighborhood. I can just hear my mind saying, 'Once again, you chose stupidly.' Maybe I have some kind of genetic lack of confidence. Even though I am doing pretty well in my life, I obsess over making decisions, and I blame myself when things go wrong."

Lots of folks were laughing by this time. They recognized that each contributor had added one of the traditional list of five hindrances: desire (sometimes called lust, which somehow sounds worse), aversion (in all its permutations from annoyance to rage), fatigue (called sloth and torpor in traditional texts), restlessness (which manifests as worry or fretting, as if the mind has more energy than it can deal with), and doubt (which often manifests as insecurity).

People were also relieved, I think, to find that other people struggled in the same ways they did. We imagined how it would be if we broke up into *kilesha* groups, affinity groups for people who recognized themselves as having any one of those five responses as their most immediate reaction to challenge. Group members, we assumed, would feel comfortable in one another's company. It's embarrassing to think oneself the only person in the world whose mind gets caught in silk pajamas, or whose anger fuse is uncomfortably short, or whose mind keeps fretting even though he or she knows that when people say "Worrying never accomplishes anything," they are right. Furthermore, group members could give one another coping suggestions. They would know coping from the inside out.

In fact, that particular class did divide into five groups that morning with, as it happened, more people choosing to be in the angry and worried groups than in the other three. I've done that exercise with many classes I've taught since that time, and the same ratio of people in groups generally holds true. I begin by giving an overview of the five energies—desire, anger, fatigue, worry, and doubt—and then I tell about my own most prominent difficulty. I worry easily. I am definitely not as much held captive by my tendency to worry as I was thirty years ago—indeed, I introduce myself as a recovering fretter—but my capacity for making up stories with dire endings still seems only a moment's careless thought away.

I describe how I used to be this way: "I would worry-worry-worry while something was happening about which the outcome was unsure, and then as soon as the tension in my mind about whatever it was caught in was over, I would think, 'All of that extra pain of worry was worthless. I see that so clearly. I'll never do that again.' And then, fifteen minutes later or the next day or pretty soon, in any event, a new fret would start." Looking around at the folks in the room as I say that, I see many heads nodding in recognition. Those people for whom another of the energies is the most troublesome use the sense of my story to identify the group that best describes them.

Perhaps the most important part of talking to other people about the tendency of the mind to fill with one or another of the afflictive emotions—in addition to its being supportive and consoling—is that it makes it clear that the "difficulty" is a habit pattern, open to change. My guess about my worrying habit is that I was born with it, or at least the tendency to have it. I can't recall not having it. I follow the newest research on neurobiology, and I'm pretty sure that geneticists will soon announce that response-to-challenge-tendencies are coded on genes along with eye color, hair texture, and the ability to carry a tune. I'm also fairly certain that the frightening events of my childhood, such as my mother's illness, or air-raid drills at school where we sat in the halls listening for planes, or citywide blackout drills at night where we turned off all the lights—although they may have exacerbated my worrying tendency—weren't responsible for it. If I had another mind, it would have come out some other way.

It's a great relief to be able accept one's own—or anyone else's—afflictive mind habits as the karmic consequence of complex, somewhat random, although always lawful circumstances. Genetics are amazing and karma is mysterious. Only one of my four children has intensely curly hair. Some of my grandchildren, born in peacetime to healthy parents, tend to fret. Some of these very same grandchildren have siblings, sharing their family experience, who don't fret. Who knows how these things get passed along through generations? The important thing is that emotional tendencies, unlike hair texture, can be modified. I know that from my own experience.

It's really true that I am a recovering fretter. I often "almost" fret, as if my tendency has left a residual track in my neurology. My mind still leaps easily to a scenario of dire consequences in response to what I interpret as challenge, but most of the time, I don't believe it. I think to myself, "There is my thought machine again, doing its thing. Who knows? Maybe this is the one time in a million that my worry turns out to be true. If it is, I'll do something about it then. Now I will not rise to the bait." I'm definitely finding that as I give less airtime to worrying, the thoughts themselves are fewer. Sometimes, when I think dire thoughts, I can even laugh. It is thrilling, after spending so much of my life held in the thrall of anxiety, to be able to delight in my mind's seemingly endless capacity for dramatic imagination. I think that perhaps it's what makes me a good storyteller.

Just as I am a recovering fretter, my friends who identify themselves as "lust types" or "aversive types" or "torpor types" (torpor is the traditional word the texts use to describe minds that are easily fatigued) or "doubt types" are also recovering. All of us go about our lives getting things done, aware of our tendencies but not held hostage by them. My friend Dick Bolton heard me tell the story about the stolen tires when I was teaching in Portland, Oregon, and when I asked people to raise their hands to indicate the type that seemed most like themselves, he said, "I don't understand this at all. I would have gone back into my apartment, phoned the police, made a report, called a taxi, and gone to work."

Of course! Most of us would do that. And all the people in all the groups at which I posed that question would have done the same. Our tendencies describe the mood the mind brings with it as it responds to challenge, not necessarily the response itself. For most of us, after some flurry, the mind settles down and we adapt to whatever is happening. Noticing "This is my habitual flurry pattern" is a big help in having the settling happen sooner. Sometimes the settling happens just from the noticing, and other times the noticing is the signal to do something as an antidote to flurry, such as taking a deep breath or just waiting.

Now let's go back to the Zen master story. For the purpose of talking about concentration as the antidote to ordinary, run-of-the-mill confusion, I'd like to replace his life-and-death challenge that demanded clarity with an everyday challenge that would have left room for his mind to be confused by contentious response. Let's suppose the monks in his monastery became unruly, disrespectful of him or of one another. Or that they all decided to find other teachers or leave monastic life. Or that the master developed arthritis in his knees and could no longer sit on his meditation cushion. If I were writing the story, I would say

the Zen master wasn't pleased with any of these develop-
ments. I'd say that he felt annoyed and disappointed. I'd say
that he felt discouraged about his leadership and that he
yearned for a more comfortable body. And that he didn't bat
an eye.

Composure as the Support for Sadness

Sadness isn't a *kilesha,* a habit pattern evoked by challenge. Sadness is what the mind feels when it is bereaved
or bereft. All the wisdom in the world about the inevitability of change or the lawfulness of *karma* does not ease the
heaviness in the mind that we feel when we lose someone,
or something, we hold dear. The mind can't think clearly
when it realizes the shape of the future has changed forever.
I remember when my aunt Miriam and I were dressing to
go to my mother's funeral—my mother had been in frail
health, but her sudden death was a surprise—I asked, "Should
we wear lipstick? Do people wear lipstick at funerals?"

"I don't know," Miriam answered. "Too bad Gladys isn't
here. She would know."

I remember that we were both startled. Of course it

was too bad Gladys wasn't there. But it was too bad because she'd died, not because we didn't know about makeup rules.

All losses are sad. The end of an important relationship is also a death. When people fall out of love with each other, or when what seemed like a solid friendship falls into ruin, the hope for a shared future—a hope that provided a context and a purpose to life—is gone. The "survivors" of a broken relationship—even when the break is "for the best"—are surprised to find themselves in a world that is suddenly different, and the mind needs to learn how to make its way in it.

The end of health or of vigor is sad. My friend Tamara, whose doctors, as I write, are trying to find a chemotherapy that will arrest her ovarian cancer, says, "This is very hard, Sylvia. I don't know what I would do without my meditation practice. Even though I can't think very well, at least I know I am breathing. Then, after I meditate Jimmy and I watch the Marlins game on TV."

Now Take a Breath:
Wise Concentration as the Universal Antidote

Take a breath right now. One long, deliberate breath that you feel from the very beginning of it until the end of it. Try it, really. You can do it with your eyes open. You can do it while reading these instructions. Do you notice that you can feel your body, and especially your chest expanding and relaxing to accommodate the air flowing in and out, without stopping reading?

Think, first of all, of concentration as developing composure. You don't need to memorize the Factors of Concentration—the five components of concentration that provide the antidotes to individual hindrance states—because what matters is that, over time and with practice, the mind gets into the habit of composing itself. It knows, out of its own innate wisdom, how to do that. I'll tell you the factors, though, because it's a neat formulation, both in the sense of making a tidy list where every afflictive state has a remedy and also in the sense that, experientially, it works. I invite you to continue reading, following the instructions for changing the emphasis of your attention, to discover each of these factors as part of your own focused mind.

Your breathing will continue as you do this (of course!), as steadily and as naturally as it was with the first breath you took when you started reading this section. And you can stop in between reading about each of the components and close your eyes to feel the sensations of the breath more closely.

The concentrated mind has an enhanced ability to notice even small details, and in the noticing, it wakes itself up from a dispirited (torporous) state. It feels like magic to have the mind pull itself together into alertness in the middle of feeling sleepy just by paying attention. It's not surprising to become suddenly awake because something dramatic happens. What I hope you'll discover now is that the mind can become brightly alert even when there is no urgency, such as right now, by bringing the attention to any specific detail of your experience. The acuity needed to recognize a small sensation vivifies the mind. Since you are already being mindful of the general movements of your breath, try to identify the precise moment at which each inhalation ends. We normally think of a breath as one continuous event, of an inhalation *becoming* an exhalation. It doesn't. An inhalation ends. Then, after a brief pause, an exhalation begins. It's a different event. If you want to feel that particular experience more clearly, close your eyes. In fact, perhaps keep your eyes closed for five breaths, noticing the distinct moments of the in/out change in the middle of each breath. Perhaps you'll find that you feel more alert at the end of those five breaths. Try it now. When you finish the five breaths, or ten if you want to try a bit longer, see if you feel more alert. (This doesn't need to be a dramatically conclusive experiment. We are only playing with shifting attention. Whatever you noticed, it's fine.)

Now we'll try five breaths (or more if you want) in which, rather than attending to one specific detail, you keep your attention on the entire cycle (inhale/pause/exhale/pause) of each complete breath. "Here comes a breath, now going through all its changes, and now it's entirely gone" is the mental narrative of this experience. Sustaining the attention over time, the texts say, keeps the mind from "wobbling" and builds a sense of confidence, the antidote to doubt. I remember realizing, with great pleasure, "I can *so* do this," and how inspired I felt. If you want to, try it now. You might want to use your fingers to count breaths. That way, you won't need to pay attention to anything other than sensations.

Now, especially if you are feeling confident—and even if you aren't—relax. You've been breathing all your life and noticing it, too. It sometimes happens that, having been given instructions to breathe attentively, the mind becomes tense and transforms what had been a neutral event into a chore. So, really, relax. Look out a window. Put a hand on your belly and feel it rise and fall as breath moves in and out of your body. In an easy way, see if you can slow down the breathing a little. You'll probably find that you feel calmer. Increased calm is one of the five Factors of Concentration, and it is the natural antidote to anxiety, to the fretful mind. Take a few more long, relaxed breaths. Notice whether you feel calmer.

The fourth quality of concentration is a heightened awareness of body sensations. Traditional Buddhist texts use the word *rapture* to describe these feelings, a word that we most associate with pleasant feelings. Indeed, the physical sensations associated with increased concentration, although they don't knock you over—as the word *rapture* might imply—are usually pleasant. People report feeling warm hands or relaxed muscles, or even feeling waves of delight course through their bodies. Other people report feeling a light tingling in their skin, as if the whole body were aroused. You might close your eyes now. Take some slow, easy breaths. *Expect* that your body will feel lovely, and then be on the alert for any new feelings you might have. Take your time. If you feel "Where *are* those feelings?" take another few breaths and smile. Probably you'll feel good. And rapture is the antidote to aversion. You can't feel wonderful and mad at the same time.

The last of the traditional list of five Factors of Concentration is "one-pointedness." You could practice this by saying to yourself, "I am only interested in my breath," and then continue bringing your attention to the experience of the breath and its accompanying descriptive narrative: "Chest expanding. Chest relaxing. Pleasant sensation. Mind cheerful." Or even, "Unpleasant sensation. Feeling too warm. Mind tense," if that was your experience. It doesn't matter what flavor the experiences are. What matters is your intention to stay present with the bare details of each current experience, renouncing any impulse to critique the experience or speculate about it or change it. As you stay with your resolve to be one-pointed in your attention, you'll notice your mind, in Alice-in-Wonderland form, offering distractions. "Think me!" say the thoughts at the edge of your awareness. You'll find, though, that the distractions soon disappear. It is as if the thoughts say, "This person's mind really means business. It won't budge!"

Do you want to try this for a while? I think you'll find that as your mind settles into a relaxed appreciation of "Just this is enough. I don't need other," it feels uncommonly content. Of all the components of concentration, one-pointedness comes closest to representing, all by itself, the end of suffering. There is no imperative in the mind, no yearning or lusting for anything to be different. You might consider, as you take these breaths, that you are practicing contentment.

I enjoy lining up the list of the Factors of Concentration

alongside the list of *kileshas* and being able to connect particular salubrious qualities of mind with the afflictive emotions for which they are, individually, the antidotes. Remember, though, that knowing how concentration works doesn't make it more effective. *That* it works is what matters. I think the lists appeal to my undergraduate college training as a chemist. I like thinking about which element neutralizes which other element. In practice, however, all of the Factors of Concentration are always present together and all act together. You don't need to think, "Hmmm . . . Let's see. I'm irritable, so I'll cultivate rapture," or "I'm sleepy; I'll be more attentive." Just take one breath and another and another, with as much attention in every way as you can. The confusion will sort itself out. Inclined in the right direction, the mind takes care of itself.

Epilogue:
Jeannette's Wisdom

So now there is only one thing left to say, and it's about inclining the mind in the right direction. I believe, absolutely, that the mind tends to clarity itself, just as the physical body tends to health, and that effort and mindfulness and concentration—all inherent qualities of consciousness—can be cultivated to the point of being self-activating when the mind is confused by challenge. I also believe that the unconfused mind tends naturally to benevolence and that being able to feel warmly and compassionately connected to oneself, to others, and to life itself is the antidote to suffering and the cause of happiness. I don't think the mind needs lots of instruction, but I do think it needs to be encouraged and continually inspired.

When I began this book, I imagined I'd end it with a few lines from the poet Emily Dickinson: "Done with the Compass— / Done with the chart! / Rowing in Eden." I thought it carried the message I wanted to deliver, the fact that warmhearted connection is our basic inclination, our greatest solace, and—having been discovered—our abiding ally. It makes peace of mind seem natural and normal, which I think it is. I think that's the message I've delivered. I realized, however, as I wrote, that my Eden—everyone's Eden—has turbulence in it and that I was presenting effort, mindfulness, and concentration techniques as charts for difficult times. And I realized how essential it is to me to have a compass. If my goal is happiness, I need to recognize the feeling "I'm not heading in the right direction," so I can initiate some corrective.

So I'll end with a line from Jeannette, a woman I bicycle with when I am in France. Jeannette is a year older than I, a longtime member of the Club Vélo de Saint Genis des Fontaines, and often takes the lead in group rides. I told her I'd heard that last year she'd had an accident and broken her leg.

"I did," she said. "In four places. I was looking back to check the riders behind me, and I skidded against a curb, right back there in the roundabout we just passed, and fell. I was in a cast for three months."

"Do you feel anxious these days when you ride through that roundabout?" I asked.

"No," she said. "I try not to think about it. And I pay more attention to the curb. And look," she added, "I had to have this pedal built up because my leg is shorter now and I otherwise couldn't balance myself. This way, I can go out with the club again, and that's what I want to do. It's not a big deal. You just have to figure out what to do so you can keep on going."

I think that's about it.

ACKNOWLEDGMENTS

I am indebted to Caroline Sutton, my editor at Ballantine, for her sage advice to me at a time when my personal life overwhelmed my ability to write and I despaired of finishing this book. "I'd wait, if I were you, Sylvia," she said. "Everything changes. Let some time pass. I think you'll feel differently."

And, I feel lucky that Tom Grady, both my friend and my literary agent, is resolutely supportive of me through the ups and downs of my life and my writing. I particularly treasure the one e-mail he sent me whose subject line reads, "Steady on . . ."

My friend Martha Ley, always the first reader of anything I wrote, died while this book was being written, but she read the first drafts of it.

Joelle Yuna, Martha's longtime life partner, helped me immeasurably during the final months of this book's completion with editorial support and with friendship.

I appreciate all my friends who listened and encouraged me for what seemed a long time as this book found its voice.

My sons and daughters and their families are always the emotional ballast of my life.

For my husband Seymour, my partner in everything and my best friend for these past fifty-five years, my most enormous gratitude.

PHOTO: © CHRISTINE ALICINO

SYLVIA BOORSTEIN, PH.D., is a co-founding teacher at Spirit Rock Meditation Center in Woodacre, California, and a senior teacher at the Insight Meditation Society in Barre, Massachusetts. A practicing psychotherapist, she is a frequent presenter at psychology training seminars and often a speaker at health and wellness conferences. She writes a regular column in *Shambhala Sun* and is the author of the national bestseller *It's Easier Than You Think; Don't Just Do Something, Sit There; That's Funny, You Don't Look Buddhist;* and *Pay Attention, for Goodness' Sake*. She and her husband divide their time between Sonoma County, California, and the south of France.